FAITH AT WORK
FOR PEGGY

by

DOROTHY MARTIN

MOODY PRESS
CHICAGO

Contents

1

Arrival in California

SITTING BESIDE JANE in the back seat of the car, Peggy leaned forward, eager to catch a glimpse of the house. Just a half hour ago she and her mother had been in the heart of the city at the train station, with Jane waving excitedly at them from behind the gates and Roger standing beside her stiff and tall in his chauffeur's uniform exactly as she remembered him. Now they were almost at Aunt Emily's and Peggy felt the excitement of anticipation building inside her.

The car moved smoothly past the low brick wall with its banks of rounded, clipped evergreens that swept their protection around the expanse of deep green lawn. As Roger slowed the car to turn into the wide circular drive, Peggy caught her breath as the sight of the beautiful, spacious house brought back vivid memories. It didn't seem possible that four years had slipped by since she had left it with barely a farewell look, so eager had she been to leave its bleak atmosphere for home. But now in one hungry gulp her eyes took in the beautiful house, the swimming pool, the tennis court, and the gardens brilliant with color in the summer sunshine. It was all just as beautiful as she had remembered. She felt as though it were welcoming her back and that she belonged here.

Then from beside her she heard her mother's low gasp, immediately controlled, as she too saw the house and gardens like rare jewels in an expensive setting. Her mother's reaction brought a tightness to Peggy's throat and a taste of fear for the month ahead. She could sense the contrast pictured in her mother's mind. Their own house, so dear to her when she had come for that visit so long ago, was just a house to her mother. Just a house with a small lawn in front and back, and room for only a narrow flower garden down the length of the garage—the garage with its door that sagged perpetually no matter how often or how carefully it was repaired. All of this was etched in her mother's mind in ugly contrast to this house which belonged to her sister, of whom she was so fiercely envious.

The nameless fears that Peggy had kept submerged ever since she had gotten Aunt Emily's graduation gift of tickets for the trip, spread through her now to dull some of the anticipation of the visit. She sharply regretted her father's insistence that they come to California, an insistence in which she had joined. She sensed that her mother's envy of her sister, which had been her companion all her married life, would feed itself on this luxury. As it grew, so would the bitterness she carried—bitterness at her sister, at the injustices of life and, of course, at God.

But there could be no turning back, for the car had circled the drive and stopped in front of the broad steps and immediately the heavy wooden door of the house swung wide. As Peggy glanced up, it was not the butler who stood there as he had done so forbiddingly those five years earlier, but Aunt Emily herself with a smile of welcome.

Peggy looked at the tall, spare figure in the simple black dress and saw not the angular figure nor the severity of the thin face, but beyond that, the changed expression in what had once been cold, bleak blue eyes. The new depth of spirit in Christ which had come so recently to Aunt Emily had turned chill into warmth, severity into kindness. Peggy opened the door and jumped out of the car, hurrying up the steps to throw her arms around her aunt with a cry of delight. "It's wonderful to see you!"

"And you," her aunt replied, hugging her in return for a moment before pulling away to look at her. "You've grown," was her only comment but the words were a compliment, Peggy knew.

Her flush of pleasure at Aunt Emily's approval suddenly drained away as turning, she saw the expression on her mother's face. The only word to adequately describe it was contempt, so strong it was almost spoken. But why? And for whom? Then it was gone swiftly as her mother, coming smoothly and lightly up to her sister, said, "Well, Emily, we are here."

"I hope the trip was not too tiring, Elizabeth."

"We managed nicely."

Peggy stood helplessly, feeling like a small child caught in the middle of a quarrel she didn't understand, as the two women went into the house and Roger carried in the bags. She turned to look at Jane who only raised her eyebrows in return and shrugged her shoulders with a helpless "There's nothing we can do about them."

Peggy turned then as a familiar voice said, "Peggy! It's good to see you. Forgive me if I exclaim over how much you've grown up."

"It's nice to see you, Miss Murphy." Peggy smiled back at her aunt's secretary, feeling surprised again that anyone so dainty and fragile could be so efficient and businesslike.

"I have to run an errand for your aunt, but you girls had better come in the house and cool off. I think cold drinks are being served. I'll see you later."

As Aunt Emily and Mrs. Andrews talked, their voices were so surfacely pleasant and their words so carefully correct that it seemed impossible that the atmosphere could be so formal and empty of any real friendliness. Peggy, listening anxiously, thought that Aunt Emily was as stiff and unbending as she had been five years ago to her when what she most needed to be now was warm and friendly. Again sharp regrets dismayed her at the thought of the long month ahead. How could they possibly live together that long with her mother's attitude of suspicion and resentment at her sister and remembered wrongs? If Aunt Emily didn't bend at all or show any softness, the visit would be wasted.

Yet Aunt Emily *was* different. She was a Christian and this would make her go beyond ordinary friendliness. Surely her mother would respond to this.

*   *   *

As the days slipped by, it was Aunt Emily's faith in Christ that seemed to annoy Mrs. Andrews most. She apparently resented that her sister, always having had everything in life that money could buy, now had this other gift of inner peace and serenity. She didn't

want it for herself—was contemptuous of it even—
but neither did she want her sister to have it.

The fact that Uncle Walter and Jane both made
it plain that they too were Christians didn't bother
Mrs. Andrews at all. In fact, Uncle Walter's prayer
before meals only seemed to amuse her, although she
very correctly bowed her head when everyone else
did. Peggy knew because she had peeked to see. As
for Jane, she and her mother were like strangers to
each other from the years of separation during which
Jane had lived with Aunt Emily. So it was not easy
to talk about a subject as personal as faith in Jesus
Christ. But it remained Aunt Emily's calm serenity
and peace and her evident belief that everyone ought
to know Christ as Saviour that Mrs. Andrews most
bitterly resented.

The first week of the visit was a succession of lazy
hours that Peggy was glad for after her busy year at
school and the hectic hours of summer work at the
store. They all went sightseeing to places Peggy knew
she would not have been interested in seeing five
years ago even if Jane and her aunt had cared enough
to take her to see them.

Coming home late Friday afternoon of the first
week, she found a note propped against the vase of
flowers on the hall table. "Lisa Vanacek called. Wants
you to call her back today if you can."

"Oh, good!" Peggy said to Jane "I've been meaning
to call her and just forgot. I wonder if Larry has gone
yet. He was going home for a visit for a week before
his parents went on their vacation."

Peggy dialed Lisa's number while she talked over
her shoulder to Jane, listened while it rang repeatedly,

then hung up. "Not home, I guess. I'm going to take a bath before dinner and then I'll try again."

Jane followed her upstairs, asking, "Is Larry through college yet?"

"He graduated at the end of summer school. He really worked like a dog to get through so soon. He went every summer and took extra courses during the year."

"Did Lisa go to college?"

"She's had a couple of years, I think. I'm really not sure. She's such a brain that even if she had to work her way through she would get along OK."

"What are they going to do now?"

"Well, the last I heard from Ann, Larry is starting seminary this fall and Lisa is going to work part-time and go to school part-time. Ann said something about their being married at Christmas. I've been terrible about writing Lisa so I've really lost track of their plans."

"I haven't seen her for a long time. Her mother still comes and does some work for us, and either Lisa or Anton comes to pick her up. She's absolutely the most beautiful person I've ever seen."

"Who? Mrs. Vanacek?" Peggy laughed as she asked.

"Well, do you suppose she was as pretty when she was young as Lisa is?" Jane asked curiously. "I mean, after all, Lisa has to get her looks from somewhere."

"It's hard to believe Mrs. Vanacek was ever slender and pretty. But I know Lisa doesn't look like her father."

Peggy went in to turn on the bath water while Jane talked. She came back into the room to hear the end of her sentence. ". . . really groovy."

"Who is?"

"Anton. He's really a sharp looker. Real dark. And tall."

"I haven't seen him for a long time of course. He must be—what? A senior?"

"Uh-huh. I've never actually spoken to him even. When he comes to get his mother he just sits out in the car, and I've never had enough nerve to go out and talk to him."

Peggy could see Jane from where she stood in front of the mirror and was surprised at the expression on her face. It was so wistful and longing and hope-less that it gave her a different picture of Jane. She was troubled again by how little she knew her own sister.

But she only said aloud, "He'd probably be glad if you did. Talk to him, I mean."

"But after I said hi, I'd be stuck. Especially if he didn't say anything back. Maybe he doesn't like it because his mother works for us and maybe he thinks I'm a snob or something."

Peggy thought Jane must really be gone on Anton or she wouldn't be so self-conscious about talking to him. One thing she had never lacked was confidence in herself.

Aloud she said, "I keep remembering Anton as just a kid when he couldn't have been much younger than I. I forget other people grow up too."

"*He* sure has," Jane said and then she got up abruptly. "I'd better get ready too. Let me know what Lisa wants."

"Wait, I'll call her again right away." Peggy dialed

again, waited a moment and then exclaimed, "Lisa! It's Peggy. How are you?"

The welcome in Lisa's voice was muted by its note of urgency as she said, "Peggy! I'm glad you're here, but I suppose it means you didn't get my letter before you left home."

"No, and there's nobody home to forward any mail." Then, in sudden alarm, she asked quickly, "Is something wrong?"

Lisa laughed softly. "No, nothing's wrong. In fact, everything is very much all right. I just wanted you to know that Larry and I are being married on Tuesday. When Ann told me you were visiting your aunt, I was so glad to know you would be able to come—"

But Peggy broke in with an excited "Lisa! I can't believe it! But how come? I mean, I think it's wonderful and I'm so excited for you. But I thought Ann said Larry was going to start seminary and get a job and you were going to wait until Christmas—"

"We were," Lisa interrupted and her voice quavered. "But Larry's been drafted so we decided we wouldn't wait. He has to leave in three weeks."

"But that's not fair! I thought he was S-2 or whatever the number is for student deferment." Her voice sputtered with indignation.

Lisa laughed a little, though her voice was shaky as she answered, "It's good to have you so defensive for us but I'm afraid it won't help any. Larry was exempt and was supposed to be for the rest of the time he was in school. But there's been a mix-up someplace apparently. I guess those things happen sometimes."

"But didn't you do something about it? I mean,

he's been planning on being a minister ever since I can remember. It isn't that he's just trying to get out of going in service. Can't you do something?"

"Larry did talk to his draft board. It was such a surprise that we were upset about it at first. He went to see them when he got the notice that he'd been reclassified, but they said he had to go. So he feels this is the Lord's plan for him."

"Yes, but how do *you* feel about it?"

"I must admit I argued about it quite a bit, but after all Larry's the one who has to go. He feels so strongly that the Lord knew all about this that he doesn't think it's right to appeal anymore. So we're going ahead with the wedding since we don't know how to plan for Christmas or any time ahead."

Then her voice quickened and lifted as she said, "And it's wonderful that you can come. I never dreamed you would be here."

"I'm glad too because I wouldn't miss your wedding for anything. Wait a minute, Lisa, Jane is making all sorts of faces at me trying to find out what this is all about. Wait a minute while I tell her."

After a moment she said, "OK, I'm back. Jane's as excited as I am. Now, when and where is it going to be?"

"At my church at eight o'clock on Tuesday. I don't have time to send out invitations so I'm just calling people and having it announced in church so we'll reach most of our friends that way. Tell Jane we want her to come. And your aunt and uncle too if they want to," she added with a hint of shyness in her voice. "And Ann said your mother is with you. I'd love to see her again."

"Don't worry, we'll all be there. Are Larry's parents coming?"

"No, that's our only regret about getting married so quickly. His dad has promised to speak at a conference in Canada and they can't get away on such short notice. We had wanted him to marry us, of course, but what can't be, can't be."

"Is there anything we can do to help?"

"I don't think so, Peg. We had everything planned for December anyway, so it's just a matter of moving things up a few months. Except for not sending out invitations, we'll do everything else we'd planned. I didn't want an elaborate wedding because Mother can't afford much and I didn't want to leave her with a lot of bills to pay by herself."

"When is Ann coming? Where is she staying?"

"She's supposed to get here Monday morning. The group she's with is singing at a church near here on Sunday and they are through after that. She didn't say how long she planned to stay."

"Can we help by putting her up here? You know we've got plenty of room."

"Well—if she'd rather," Lisa answered slowly. "But —well, I was counting on her staying at my house. It would give Mother someone to talk to after I'm gone."

"Of course. I'm sorry, Lisa. I was just being selfish in wanting to talk to Ann myself."

"I'd like her to bridge the lonely hours Mother will have for a few days after I'm gone. You know Ann. She'll say and do the right thing to help without knowing she is. Mother doesn't think she will need anyone because she has Anton. But he can't do for her what Ann can."

Peggy didn't dare ask Lisa about her father. If he had become a Christian, Lisa would have said so; if he were not, it was better not to ask questions and shadow Lisa's happiness.

So she said, "Tell Ann to call when she gets here. And if there is *anything* we can do, you know we will. Just ask for anything you need."

"Thanks, Peggy, I will."

As Peggy put down the receiver, she shook her head at the thought of prickly Mrs. Vanacek needing anyone to be company to her. *I'm glad it's Ann who has to do it and not me,* she thought with relief.

And yet, to have had Lisa in your life and then to lose her even in a happy marriage would make anyone lonely. Especially if you were left with only a young son and a drunken slob for a husband. She wondered if Mr. Vanacek would come to the wedding. Could he stay sober long enough?

2

Lisa's Wedding

AUNT EMILY was delighted with the news of Lisa's wedding and was determined to do something to help.

"Mrs. Vanacek has worked for me too long for me not to know how stubbornly proud she is. I'm sure she can't afford to do very much for Lisa, yet she won't let anyone help her because she would consider that it was being done out of charity instead of affection."

She paused and looked at Peggy and then away as she added sadly, almost as though the words were forced from her, "I must help. I have so much to atone for." Remembering the past and her aunt's haughty disdain of Mrs. Vanacek, Peggy didn't have to ask any questions.

Instead she covered the awkward moment by saying, "Lisa said they didn't need anything because they weren't planning an elaborate wedding. But I do wish we could do something for her besides giving a gift. I know what you mean about her mother though. She'd get mad if you offered her any help."

Her aunt frowned thoughtfully, tapping her fingers on the arm of the chair. "Is this wedding going to be in her church?"

Peggy nodded.

"There is something we can do then. Every wedding, no matter how simple it is, needs flowers. And we have plenty. I'll call her."

Peggy waited while her aunt dialed the number, eager to hear how the clash of two such strong personalities would turn out. She smiled to herself that Aunt Emily couldn't see that she was just like Mrs. Vanacek in the matter of pride and stubbornness.

She listened as her aunt said, "Lisa? This is Mrs. Conway. Peggy has just been telling me the good news about your forthcoming marriage. We are delighted to hear of it and appreciate your invitation to attend. We will plan to come. . . . . Now, may I speak to your mother? . . . Mrs. Vanacek, Mrs. Conway here. Tell me what color flowers Lisa wants for her church decorations and I'll have the gardener bring them to the church Tuesday morn— . . . . What? . . . Yes, I know you can manage. . . . Of course I understand you can take care of the arrangements yourself. . . . Mrs. Vanacek, we have flowers going to waste in the garden, and there is no reason Lisa shouldn't have them. . . . I know you don't need them, but this is a gift to Lisa. . . . A wedding gift. . . . Yes, I'm only doing this for Lisa," she repeated firmly.

She covered the mouthpiece, shaking her head as she looked at Peggy. "She's asking Lisa about the colors. Such a stubborn woman!"

Peggy bit the insides of her cheeks to keep back the laughter as her aunt continued to shake her head in exasperation and then listened again. "Yellow and white? Very well. We have plenty of roses. Peggy and Jane will come along on Tuesday and we'll have the flowers at the church in time for Lisa to arrange them as she wishes. . . . Thank you. Good-bye."

She hung up and looked at Peggy. "I hope you don't mind my arranging your day for you Tuesday. With stubborn people like that, you simply have to go ahead and do what is best for them in spite of their objections. Mrs. Vanacek has been so accustomed to working for everything all her life, she doesn't know how to accept a gift, poor soul."

"I'll do anything to help Lisa," Peggy answered. But at the same time, she was glad her mother hadn't been there to hear her sister in action. This kind of officiousness, as her mother called such help, was what she hated most in anyone, and it would be especially hard for her to forgive this in Aunt Emily.

But when she discovered Tuesday morning that her aunt intended that she and Jane were to help Lisa decorate the church, she panicked and pleaded, "Please help us, Mother. You know I don't know how to decorate anything!"

"Neither do I," Jane chimed in.

"It's really Lisa's affair after all," their mother replied tartly. "You don't even know she wants the flowers since I understand from what has been said that neither she nor her mother had anything to say about the idea."

"Oh, Lisa's glad to have them. But she won't be if she has to count on me to help her fix them."

"You don't even know that she needs help. She probably is capable of doing anything she wants to."

"Just come with us anyway and see," Peggy begged.

"Well, I'll come," Mrs. Andrews finally agreed reluctantly. "But if Lisa has her own ideas, I have no intention of interfering. You know how I dislike officious people."

"I know she'll be glad for your help," Peggy insisted.

And she was. She was waiting in front of the church when they pulled up and got out of the car, and she exclaimed, "Oh, Mrs. Andrews, I've been hoping you would come. I need your help. I know what I want but doing it just right is my problem."

"I'll do what I can," Mrs. Andrews answered, and Peggy gave an inward sigh of relief at the warmth and graciousness of her mother's voice.

Lisa led them into the church as she explained, "Larry made a trellis and painted it white and we wanted to cover it with greens and then put flowers on it at various places." She looked at Mrs. Andrews anxiously.

"That shouldn't be too hard." Mrs. Andrews looked at the trellis critically. "But you should balance it with several baskets of flowers on each side and then place several baskets of greens along here. We brought plenty with us. Girls, go out and help bring in the things."

Jane came back with her arms full of flowers and asked, "Who are all those people going in and out of the basement?"

"The most wonderful people in the world," Lisa replied with shining eyes. "They're the mothers of the girls in my Sunday school class. They've offered to make sandwiches and cookies for the reception. Mother was glad for the help because she's baking the wedding cake and would really have been pushed for time if she had to do everything else."

Peggy and Jane hid their smiles at Lisa's version of her mother's eagerness for help, wondering if these ladies had just insisted the way Aunt Emily had.

But Lisa finished tremulously, "I just can't believe how nice everyone has been to help us get ready."

Larry came up from the basement in time to hear the last of the sentence. He hugged her. "People are nice to people who are nice," he said and then added, "Hi, Peggy, how are you? Mrs. Andrews, it's been a long time since I've seen you. How's Bill?"

"We haven't the slightest idea," Mrs. Andrews replied tartly. "He and his father are so busy looking after waifs they don't have time to write to their family."

"Bill and my dad are at the same place Bob is," Peggy explained hastily. "Bill has been there all summer and Dad went down just for this month. They're probably kept plenty busy."

"And we must get busy too if we expect to finish in time," Mrs. Andrews broke in abruptly. "I'll need you girls, so come along."

Actually Peggy and Jane didn't do anything but stand around and hand things to whoever asked for them and run up and down stairs on errands. Then they began exclaiming at the way the front of the church was being transformed under Mrs. Andrews' skilled touch.

"It's beautiful!" Lisa exclaimed when finally the job was done to Mrs. Andrews' satisfaction and they all stood back to look at the result. "How can I ever thank you?"

Mrs. Andrews shrugged. "You'd better thank the one who sent the flowers. I only worked with what belonged to someone else."

The bitterness in her voice was unmistakable and Peggy and Jane looked at each other in dismay. But

Lisa only smiled at her and said softly, "But you gave more than things; you gave your skill—and love." The last word held the whisper of a question.

After a moment Mrs. Andrews, to Peggy's utter surprise, said, "Yes, I believe I do love you," and she leaned over and gave Lisa's cheek a fleeting kiss.

"That's a wish for your happiness," she said as she turned away. "Now, girls, get things gathered up. It's past lunchtime. And, Lisa, you'd better go home and get some rest."

"I will. And thanks so much!"

Peggy turned to Lisa, her mind whirling with emotions that were too complex to sort out except for the amazement she felt at her mother's demonstration of affection for Lisa. She blinked back tears as she said, "I'll see you tonight, Lisa. You too, Larry."

"Bye, gals. Thanks for all the help. Don't expect me to recognize anyone tonight except Lisa," he said as he smiled down at her.

Uncle Walter had to leave unexpectedly that afternoon for an out-of-town business engagement so Aunt Emily had Roger drive them to the church.

As they got out of the car, Aunt Emily said, "I'm sure you would be welcome, Roger, if you want to come in to the ceremony, unless you would rather go home and then come back for us. I have no idea how long we will be."

He touched his cap. "Thank you. I'll come in if it's all right. I know what Mrs. Vanacek thinks of her daughter, and I know what a fine person she is. I'd like to see her wedding."

"It *is* beautiful, Elizabeth," Peggy heard her aunt

say as they entered the church and stood looking down the length of the center aisle.

And it was. The pale yellow roses against the green of the ivy in the trellis was perfect. The candles were already lighted and the slim pencils of light flickered gently in the breeze coming in the open window. A number of people were already seated. As they waited, Anton came over to them. "Lisa wants you to sit up front," he said, offering Aunt Emily his arm.

As they followed him down the aisle, Peggy looked at him and thought how right Jane was. He was dark —and tall—and very good-looking. "He really *is* groovy," she whispered and wasn't surprised to see Jane's face get red as she gave a short nod in reply.

The church was practically filled as far as Peggy could tell without looking around too much. Before Anton had ushered them down the aisle, she had noticed four or five girls sitting together on one side of the church. She turned her head to look at them again. From their appearance, she wondered if this was the first time any of them had been in church, and she couldn't help wondering what connection they had with Lisa.

Then, as the wedding march began, she stood with everyone else to watch Lisa come down the aisle on Anton's arm. Momentarily she was diverted from Lisa's glowing face as she thought how sad it was that it was her brother and not her father walking with her. She wondered if they had even told him about the wedding or if he cared enough to be told.

In the hush of the church, the beautiful promises of the marriage ceremony were given and received in clear, confident tones. The words mingled with

Peggy's memories of the past when the romance had begun. The long-ago Christmas when Lisa had visited them with Jane came back to her now. Her lips curved in a smile as she remembered how she had thought her world was shattered when Larry fell in love with Lisa that Christmas. But there could be no doubt of the rightness of the marriage or of their love for each other. Its depth was measured in the feeling in Larry's voice as he pledged himself to Lisa forever and in the confidence in her sweet voice as it came clearly in reply. Peggy found herself torn between tears and smiles as she listened.

Even Aunt Emily's eyes were a little misty as the ceremony ended and they turned with the rest of the guests to watch the bride and groom leave. Peggy stood with Jane and her mother and aunt in the long line that inched along the aisle and then gradually down the stairs to the church basement. She wished they did not form such a tight little group of strangers and was wondering what to say to the people behind them when she heard a familiar voice exclaim, "Peggy, is it really you?"

She turned. "Mrs. Tremont! How wonderful to see you! You haven't changed a bit."

"You certainly have," Mrs. Tremont laughed in admiration. "You're just as pretty as you used to be, but you've grown up amazingly."

"You're flattering me," Peggy protested. "You know my aunt, Mrs. Conway, don't you? And I'd like you to meet my mother. Mother, this is one of my most favorite teachers."

"Now who's doing the flattering?" Mrs. Tremont laughed. "Isn't this a wonderful day for Lisa? They are such an unusual couple." She smiled at Mrs. Andrews. "Lisa tells me she owes your family a great deal. She said if she hadn't visited you, she never would have met Larry."

"She would have met someone else then," Mrs. Andrews answered, looking across the room at Lisa. "She's far too beautiful to have remained single."

"Yes, but would anyone else have been right for her?" Mrs. Tremont asked. "I'm a firm believer that marriages are made in heaven."

Mrs. Andrews' smile touched only her lips as she retorted coldly, "It's a pity that heaven makes so many mistakes then."

"This one is certainly no mistake," Peggy broke in hastily.

Jane added quickly, "They're just perfect for each other."

Peggy was grateful that Mrs. Tremont changed the subject by asking, "By the way, do you remember Sally Sanders, by any chance?"

"Yes, of course, I went to a slumber party at her house once. How is she?"

She noticed that Mrs. Tremont hesitated, exchanged just the barest of glances with Jane, and then answered briefly, "Grownup. If you think of it, pray for her. She needs it."

Mrs. Andrews looked at Mrs. Tremont, her surprise at the answer showing plainly, but there was no chance to say anything more for they had reached Lisa and Larry and went through the brief reception line. Peggy noticed the simplicity and dignity with which Mrs. Vanacek thanked everyone for coming even though she knew very few of the people personally.

She had refused to leave the ritual of her own church for the informality of this one even though she had accepted the Lord as her Saviour.

Ann caught the bride's bouquet which Lisa tossed directly to her with a lightly blown kiss before she and Larry turned to slip out the door. Peggy hadn't noticed that Anton had not been around until she saw him come in a few minutes later with several friends and head for the food. Mrs. Vanacek said something to him to which he shook his head reassuringly and Peggy saw his mother turn away with an unmistakable sigh of relief.

"He has been watching Larry's car to be sure it was safe," she said, answering the question in Peggy's look.

Many of the guests were leaving and Peggy wondered how much longer her mother would keep her disinterest and impatience from showing now that Lisa and Larry had gone. Probably Aunt Emily would want to leave soon too, so she asked Mrs. Vanacek, "Is there anything we can do to help you before we leave?"

"I do not know where to put all the gifts." She frowned down at the table which was loaded with packages. "I cannot take them all home; they would not be safe."

Jane, hearing her, whispered, "What does she mean?"

But Peggy shook her head in warning and whispered back, "Find out if we could store them for her."

Jane went over to Aunt Emily who listened to what she said, nodded, and came over to Mrs. Vanacek.

"Can we be of any assistance? Would you like Roger to help Anton carry the packages to the car?"

Mrs. Vanacek hesitated and before she could answer, Aunt Emily went on smoothly, "Perhaps we could even store some of them for you. We have plenty of room, you know, and we could keep them until Lisa comes home and decides what she wants to do about them."

"That might be best. At least they would be safe," Mrs. Vanacek agreed reluctantly.

Peggy marveled again at how graciously Aunt Emily was able to smooth over awkward moments. Then she remembered that she had always been like this. Even when Peggy hadn't liked her—had almost hated her, in fact—on that first visit, she had sensed this ability Aunt Emily had to do the outwardly correct thing. And now, of course, the ability was combined with a genuine spirit of love and a desire to help because she was a Christian.

Anton came in again, followed this time by Roger who was very agitated and said to Aunt Emily in a low voice, "This is a pretty rough neighborhood. I've had to keep a close watch on the car. Some of the boy's friends are out there now on guard."

But Mrs. Vanacek had overheard and said to him with a short hard laugh, "This is not the kind of neighborhood you are used to. It is better that Anton stays out there as long as the car is here."

Several of the ladies who were clearing the tables stopped to listen and one of them nodded her head vigorously. "It's getting so that none of us dares to be out on the streets after dark. This used to be a good neighborhood—not fancy, you understand—but good. And safe. But not anymore. It's changed. The people who live here have changed. It's a different class coming in here now."

Peggy glanced at Aunt Emily, wondering what she was thinking as they stood listening to the conversation.

"Not upper class like us," Mrs. Vanacek said then with her abrupt laugh.

"You know what I mean," the other woman retorted. "We're decent people. We don't have much but we're decent. Our husbands work and we don't expect a handout from anybody. We're law-abiding. We're not riffraff even if we are poor. And that's what's moving in here now—riffraff. They don't want an honest day's work. They just want to loaf and have people who do work take care of them. And they let their kids run wild too. If my kids acted the way some of theirs do, I'd wallop them good."

"And they're just out for themselves, too, no matter what they say when they hang around decent kids at school and try to get them all stirred up." The other women were all nodding their heads in vigorous agreement with the two who had spoken up.

Peggy, turning then from the boxes of towels she had stacked together, caught the troubled look on Ann's face and looked at her curiously.

"What's the matter? You look as though you have a problem."

"I have, Peg, kind of. Can we talk sometime in the next couple of days?"

"Sure, but I didn't think you were staying very long. Or maybe I didn't understand Lisa since I was so excited about her news."

"I was planning to join my folks in Canada for a

week before going back to school."

"Is that a past tense I hear?"

Ann frowned thoughtfully. "Yes, I think so. That's mostly what I want to talk to you about. When can I see you?"

Peggy looked to see if Mrs. Vanacek were within hearing distance before she said, "I wish you could come home with us tonight but I know Lisa wants you to stay with her mother."

"And I really want to. She's a dear down under all that exterior fierceness, and she's going to miss Lisa terribly. She's had such a horrible life—still has, for that matter. If it weren't for Lisa and Anton I don't know how she'd have stood it all these years. Nothing seems to reach Mr. Vanacek at all."

"I know," Peggy said soberly and couldn't resist a glance at her mother sitting by herself, an amused smile on her lips as she watched Aunt Emily gather up ribbons and wrappings.

Ann followed her look and said contritely, "I'm sorry, Peg. I know you can sympathize more with Lisa and her mother than I can although Mr. Vanacek is in such an awful drunken state all the time." After a moment she went on, "Let me just tell you this much now—" She stopped as Jane joined them, and then said, "I don't suppose Lisa had a chance to tell you about this club she has started."

"No, what kind of a club? Who's it for?"

There was a sudden commotion in the street outside and they could hear Anton loudly shout, "Beat it or I'll bust you one."

Then Roger yelled, "Clear out, all of you, or we'll call the police."

Ann smiled faintly as she looked back at Peggy and answered, "With the riffraff."

Peggy looked at her. "I don't get it—"

But Jane, listening, interrupted. "Is that why Aunt Emily wanted me to go through my clothes for anything I'd outgrown or didn't want because Lisa wanted them for somebody she knew?"

Ann nodded. "She's really been bothered by all the kids in her neighborhood that the church wasn't reaching in any way. This is really an active church with lots of things going on, and the kids who come really like it and keep on coming. But there were new families moving into her neighborhood and they were —" She hesitated and then, with a shrug of her shoulders, finished, "The riffraff, I guess, like that woman said. And none of them would come to church to see if they liked it or not."

"How did Lisa get to know them?" Peggy asked, remembering the five girls who had sat together during the ceremony upstairs.

"She just was friendly to them. You know how Lisa is. For example, a family moved into her block with a lot of kids. Two of them were twin girls about fourteen, I think she said. She saw them sitting on their front steps one day and went over and talked to them. Then she did things like fixing their hair and so on, and of course they were crazy about her. And then they'd come over and sit on her front steps. Pretty soon other girls came. Everything was very informal and Lisa never preached at them, but she always explained to them how they could be saved. Always. Because she said otherwise what use was there in getting together and talking if sometime during the conversation they didn't talk about the most important thing in the world, which is how to become a Christian?"

"And her mother didn't mind having them hang around?"

"Yes, she did. But she'd do almost anything for Lisa, you know. And she always tried to keep Mr. Vanacek out of the way if he was home. Of course the girls knew about him. They'd see him coming home drunk all the time. Maybe that was one reason they opened up for Lisa," Ann finished thoughtfully. "They could see she had the same kind of homelife they did."

"And this is what Lisa wants to get you into?" Peggy asked.

"Yes, and I'm scared to death I'll make a mess of it."

"You don't have to do it, do you?" Jane asked.

"No, I don't have to. Except that there's nobody else to do it." Ann stooped then to pick up the few remaining boxes and said, "I guess we'd better go. We're keeping everyone else waiting."

They stepped out into the soft evening air and Peggy looked around a little nervously. Down the street a record player was blaring, competing with several TVs which were going full blast in other houses. A group of small boys who should have been home in bed were playing marbles under a streetlight on the corner. Whoever Anton and Roger had yelled at earlier must have gone without any trouble, though Roger was still standing on guard by the right front door of the car. She laughed at herself for her uneasy feelings and thought that Roger too was being unnecessarily melodramatic.

But the uneasy feeling returned later when they were in the car. Roger, following Anton's old car, pulled to the curb in front of the Vanacek house and Peggy saw how much the neighborhood had changed for the worse in the few years since she had visited there. The Vanacek house itself was greatly improved, for it had obviously been recently painted. But the general tone of the surroundings was one of despair and neglect. A broken window in the barbershop across the street had been repaired by a piece of plywood rather than glass; a sagging fence with broken slats ran the length of the house next door; a rusty car parked halfway down the street looked as though it had been in that spot for a long time.

How awful for Lisa to have lived here all her life! What a contrast it must be for Mrs. Vanacek to go out to Aunt Emily's to work and then to come home to this!

But as Peggy looked around at all the decay, she became aware of the anxiety on Anton's face as he got out of his car and looked up at the house. Lights were on in all the rooms, and the neighbors were standing curiously on their front porches as Roger got out of the car and went around to open the door for Mrs. Vanacek. She glanced up at the house impassively. But Peggy, looking too, caught her breath as she saw the figure swaying in the open doorway, framed in the light from the hall. Then Mrs. Vanacek leaned down to say to Aunt Emily, "I will let you know what Lisa wants to do about the gifts. I think they will be back in a week."

"We'll keep them as long as necessary," Aunt

Emily replied. Then looking up toward the house, she asked anxiously, "Could Roger—"

Mrs. Vanacek shook her head. "I have Anton," she said proudly, straightening and turning toward the house. As she reached the porch, those waiting in the car saw her husband lean forward and grab her shoulder. But Anton was there at once and, taking hold of his father, he turned him around and led him inside while Mrs. Vanacek followed.

No one said anything as Roger pulled away from the curb and drove quickly along the street. Peggy wondered if everyone else felt as sad and hopeless as she did. She couldn't see her mother's face and was sure it would not reveal her thoughts anyway. But glimpsing her aunt's profile in the light of the street-lamps, she suddenly felt the burden on her heart eased a little. The situation wasn't as hopeless as it seemed because miracles did take place whether you expected them or not.

If anyone had needed proof of Aunt Emily's changed heart, this evening was the proof. For Aunt Emily's social barriers to crumble so that she could speak to her laundress as an equal and bring her home as a friend, was a miracle only God could bring about. Surely her mother must see how much better the new Aunt Emily was.

Yet, she couldn't see it by herself. It had taken the power of Christ to change her aunt and it would take that for her mother too. He was the only one who could make Aunt Emily of the social register a sister in spirit to her laundress, the wife of a drunkard. And only He could melt the bitterness that held her mother's heart.

3

An Unexpected Phone Call

LYING COMFORTABLY and lazily beside the pool several days later, Peggy yawned and said, "I've just got to get some letters written, but I can't get enough ambition to do them."

"I wouldn't bother," Jane answered, yawning in return. "Probably nobody will answer anyway."

"Alice will and she's the one I promised to write to."

"She's probably glad you haven't written so she doesn't have to answer."

"No, that's a funny thing about Alice. She's got this determined streak in her so if she has to do something she does it no matter what."

"You got a letter from somebody yesterday."

Peggy opened her eyes, grinned at Jane, and said, "OK, nosey, so I did. From Dan."

"You like him, huh?"

"He's pretty terrific, though I haven't always thought so," Peggy admitted as pictured memories of Dan flitted through her mind.

"I guess he isn't like he used to be, sort of stuck-up."

"No, he's really different. Last year was pretty awful for him—for all of us who knew him. I was really afraid he'd gone off the deep end for sure and never would really commit himself to the Lord. But he changed right at the end of school and he's—terrific."

"You sound serious about him."

"Well, I don't know for sure," Peggy answered slowly. "I thought I was serious about John last year too, but now we're just friends."

"Where is Dan going to college?"

"Same place Ann and Bob are. He applied so late he was really surprised that he was accepted. Fortunately he had high grades which helped."

"It would be neat if you and he were going the same place."

"In a way I'm glad we're not," Peggy answered thoughtfully. "We're not that sure yet about anything for the future and this will give us a chance to date other people."

"Did you go with many guys while you were in high school?"

Peggy shook her head. "I liked Larry an awful lot when I was young, but I never had a date with him. John was the first one I ever really dated." She looked at Jane and asked, "What about you?"

Jane slowly shook her head in answer. Then, abruptly changing the subject, she asked, "Have you heard from Bill or Dad since you came?"

Peggy sat up abruptly. "Hey, we haven't! How long have we been here? Two weeks?"

"Ten days. That's not so long for them not to write if they're busy."

"Yes, but Dad would certainly write to Mother. You don't suppose she got a letter and just didn't say anything about it?"

Peggy looked at Jane, who shook her head and

shrugged, "Don't ask me. You know Mother better than I do."

The words came as a shock to Peggy, partly because Jane said them so casually. But, after all, she had probably many times faced the fact that she was not a part of the family into which she had been born. The many years of separation during which Jane had lived with Aunt Emily would always keep them strangers to one another.

Then Jane said, "Here comes Mother now. Ask her if she's heard from Dad."

The girls watched their mother cross the lawn toward them. Her slender figure was stiffly erect, making her almost arrogant in appearance.

"Peggy, you're getting red across your shoulders. Be careful or you'll burn," Mrs. Andrews admonished as she sat down in one of the lace-iron chairs and pulled off her gloves.

"I've got lots of lotion on," Peggy answered. "How was the luncheon?"

Her mother shrugged. "As women's luncheons go it was typical—chicken salad and hot rolls, coffee and sherbet. Naturally I didn't know any of your aunt's friends, though I must admit they made an effort to be friendly."

Then the tone of cool disapproval in her voice deepened as she added, "The luncheon was very nice but the program, I think it was called, was long and, in part, quite unnecessary. I never have been able to understand why some people must turn every social gathering into a propaganda preaching service. Someone always feels compelled to bare his soul to people who have no choice but to sit and listen."

Peggy and Jane exchanged a quick glance. They knew how much their aunt had hoped their mother would respond to the Christian witness that was always a part of the program of this monthly luncheon meeting. But apparently it had had just the opposite effect and had irritated her.

Since it wouldn't accomplish anything to argue about it, Peggy said, "We were just saying that we haven't heard from Bill since we got here. Have you had a letter from Dad?"

"No, but I didn't expect them to think of us," Mrs. Andrews answered. "I warned Bill when he was so eager to go that he wouldn't have a bit of rest all summer, but he would go. I'm sure he spends every minute working for people who probably never thank him."

"He really likes to help people—" Jane began timidly, but her mother only shook her head disapprovingly.

"You can carry that trait to an extreme, and that is just what Bill does. He'll be worn out from the summer and not be ready for school, and with no money to show for his hard work either. And your father had no business going down there this month and working himself to death for people he doesn't know and will never see again. At least I hope neither of them pursues this foolish idea another year."

"Dad doesn't think of it as work," Peggy objected. "He was looking forward to it. You know he and Bill talked about it as though it would be a vacation."

Mrs. Andrews drew her lips into a thin line as she shook her head again. "Please don't argue with me about it, Peggy. I know you backed Bill in this foolish project when he first got the notion. I know you thoroughly approve of what they are doing and you know I don't, so there is no point in discussing it further."

When her mother was in that frame of mind and used that tone of voice, Peggy knew it was better to change the subject. So with a slight warning shake of her head at Jane, she said, "When we go shopping tomorrow, I want to look for clothes for school."

"I wish I were going to college this year," Jane said enviously. "Two more years of high school yet. Yuk!"

"Are you going out for cheerleading again?"

"Yeah, I've already made it. We have tryouts in the spring for those who have already been cheering."

"I wish I'd been a cheerleader," Peggy said wistfully.

"Did you try out?"

Peggy shook her head. "I knew it wouldn't be any use. I'd never have made it—"

"That's silly," Jane interrupted impatiently. "You don't know until you try."

"I know about this," Peggy insisted. "I'm too self-conscious. I couldn't forget myself enough to really cheer. I'd be sure everyone was seeing my mistakes."

"You have to forget about yourself," Jane said, still impatiently.

"I know. But that's not easy for me to do."

Peggy looked across at Jane as she answered. She was beginning now to see the physical resemblances between them that other people always exclaimed about, resemblances that had not been so apparent when they were younger. But she knew the similarities were only on the outside; inside they were very different.

And I'm glad I'm me, she thought contentedly. She lay drowsily in the sun, half listening to her mother

and Jane talk, and letting her mind drift lazily back
through the years. How wonderfully everything had
turned out for her all through life. God had worked
out so many impossible situations and brought her so
many friends.

There was Alice, who would always be her best
friend no matter how many years or miles or experiences separated them. And Ellen. And Ann—John—
Bob—Phyllis—Candy—Dan. Every one of them had
had an encounter with God that had completely
changed them, and changed them so much that everyone could see it. She thought of Dan's last letter and
smiled to herself, warmed by his words. She hadn't
been entirely truthful to Jane because Dan seemed to
be very sure of his feelings. He had been a part of
her life ever since she had started junior high, and it
was obvious from the way he wrote that he wanted to
be a part of it forever.

And of course she couldn't forget what God had
done for Dad and Jane and Aunt Emily and Uncle
Walter, as well as for Bill and herself. Only her mother
was left, and Peggy shied away from the painful
thought. This had been a burden to her all of her growing years, and it was no closer to being lifted.

"What are you thinking about so hard?"

Peggy, far away in thought, came back with a start
as she realized Jane had asked the question twice with
voice and eyes that were curious. She and her mother
were looking at her, waiting for an answer.

"Oh—people."

She knew better than to tell her thoughts in front
of her mother and antagonize her even more. She

wasn't even sure she felt close enough to Jane to confide in her.

Then, aware that they were both still looking at her and expecting more of an answer, she asked, "Don't you sometimes wish you could look ahead and see what's coming and know what you'll be like and what you'll be doing ten or fifteen years from now?"

Jane's "I never thought of it" and their mother's "You're better off not knowing" came at the same time and almost in the same tone of voice.

Peggy looked at them. It was strange how much alike they were. Mrs. Andrews had never had to be practical about anything while she was growing up, and neither had Jane, and yet a streak of practicality was their strongest characteristic. Neither of them ever took wild flights of fancy about anything. They always seemed to stand back and look at all sides of a question and then decide on the safest thing to do.

It was Dad who had the wild flights of fancy. It wasn't that he was foolishly impractical. But he could always see the romance and excitement and fun side of a situation, and he was willing to try something even if he wasn't exactly sure how it would turn out. That had been so obvious five years ago when he had decided to leave his job as a salesman, which he hated, and go into teaching, which he loved and was so good at. Then it had seemed like such a foolish, impossible step; looking back, anyone could see what a wise decision he had made.

But Peggy frowned now as she remembered that it was her mother who had been the most willing for him to take the risk when he had been reluctant to do it for fear it might not work out. It was her mother who had voluntarily taken a job—something entirely foreign and distasteful to her—in order to help make ends meet while her father went back to school for a year.

She sighed. People didn't always react the way you expected they would. Life was really complicated when you came right down to it, especially when you realized how much each person needed everyone else. Nobody could stand alone, no matter who they were.

Not even Mother, Peggy thought as she watched her go toward the house. The hard thing was making her realize that she did need other people's help and especially God's help. She closed her eyes again and drifted in troubled thought until her mother, coming back with some knitting, said, "You're wanted on the telephone, Peggy. It's Ann."

"Oh, good. Thanks." Peggy shrugged into a robe and went to the house, taking the call on the extension phone just off the breakfast room.

"Hi, Peggy. Is that invitation to spend the night still open?"

"Sure is. Tonight?"

"Yes. I've already told Mrs. Vanacek I'd be staying with you tonight, but I want to come back here tomorrow. I've got so many things to talk to you about."

"How will you get here?"

"Anton said he'd drive me over."

"Can you come in time for dinner?"

"Uh-uh. Anton works and can't bring me until after supper. Anyway, I don't want to. Mrs. Vanacek is cooking something I don't want to miss. She's been at it all afternoon, and you should smell the heavenly smell. I'm drooling."

"OK," Peggy laughed. "Put some of whatever it is in your pocket and come right afterward."

She hung up and turned from the phone just as it rang again.

She picked it up. "Hello?"

There was a brief silence and then a voice said, "Is Peggy Andrews there?"

"This is Peggy."

"Oh, hi. This is Sally Sanders. Remember me from way back when?"

"Sally! How are you? Of course I remember you. In fact, I saw Mrs. Tremont just a couple of days ago and she mentioned you."

"Yeah? What did she say?"

Peggy was puzzled by the hostile tone of voice and decided she hadn't better quote Mrs. Tremont. Instead she answered, "Nothing, really. She asked if I remembered you and I said I did. Why?"

"Nothing. I just wondered. I didn't think you'd remember me."

"Well I do. How are you?"

"OK. Glad I'm not in school and can be my own boss."

Peggy laughed. " 'No more teacher's dirty looks,' " she quoted. "I know what you mean, though I suppose I'd miss school if I weren't going to college."

"None of that for me."

"What are you doing?"

"Working. This is my day off so I thought I'd call you. How long are you staying?"

"A couple more weeks. But how did you know I was here?"

"I saw Jane downtown a long time ago and remembered that she was related to you. So I asked about you. Did she tell you?"

"No—"

"That figures." The bitter note was definitely there this time, and Peggy frowned over the reason for it. But Sally went on, "Anyway, when I found out you were coming out this summer, I thought I'd look you up for kicks."

"Well, look—" Peggy said quickly, because it sounded from Sally's voice like she was going to hang up. "Can't we meet someplace?"

"Well—if you want to. When?"

"You decide. I'm on vacation and don't have to punch a time clock."

"How about meeting me for lunch on my day off next week—Wednesday?"

"OK, where?"

While Sally tried to decide, Peggy was thinking of the happy confusion of Sally's family when she had gone to her house for the slumber party and stayed for breakfast after the other girls went home. Remembering the closeness of the family and the fun they had had with each other, she broke in impulsively, "I'd love to see your folks again, even though they wouldn't remember me. Your sisters were so cute. Especially the youngest one who kept coming up to remind you of things you were supposed to do and then running down and reporting to your mother that we were just 'lying around doing nothing.' Remember? I can't think of their names, but they all had pigtails and were so cute. And you called them all monsters— affectionately, of course."

"Yeah."

The voice was flat and disinterested, even cold, and Peggy was sharply aware that something was wrong with Sally, something that had to do with her family.

Then Sally spoke abruptly and curtly. "Look, do you remember where Groton's department store is? Jane can tell you. Meet me there and we'll go someplace to eat."

"What time? Twelve? One?"

"One, I guess. I don't get around too early on my day off. Oh, will I know you? I mean, you haven't changed, have you? Your hair color or anything?"

"No, I'm still an ordinary dull brown."

"Well, I'm not. Look for a blonde, OK?"

"Will do. It'll be fun seeing you again, Sally."

"Yeah? Maybe." And the phone clicked.

Peggy put down the receiver slowly and stood thinking of the conversation and the way Sally had sounded. She wondered if she was remembering the same girl after all. It had been so long since they had known each other for such a brief time. Something was wrong, and Mrs. Tremont's words were beginning to take on meaning.

She went out through the French doors from the breakfast room and stopped as she saw Jane coming toward the house. How to find out anything from Jane was always a problem because she could be pretty stingy about passing on information.

"That was a long phone call," Jane said as Peggy turned to go back into the house with her.

"Two of them. The first was Ann, and she's coming over after dinner."

"Good."

"Jane, what's wrong with Sally Sanders?" Peggy asked, watching Jane's face for a reaction.

"What made you think of her?"

"I just talked to her on the phone. She called right after Ann hung up."

"Oh."

"Don't stall, Jane. She sounded different, and I saw you and Mrs. Tremont look at each other the other day when she was talking about Sally."

Peggy waited and, after a moment, Jane said, "I've heard things about her but I don't know how much is true and how much is rumor. I guess she was in some trouble last year in school."

"What kind of trouble?"

"Some kids were suspended for smoking in the washroom and cutting too many classes. Things like that."

"I can't imagine Sally doing that," Peggy said slowly.

"As I said, I don't know all the details. You know how big stories can get the oftener they're told. Maybe Sally wasn't in on everything, but she did run around with the group that got arrested."

"Arrested! For what?"

"Well, there was a big scare in the newspapers about the increase in drugs in schools and there was a crackdown on kids who smoked. And I guess they found quite a few who weren't smoking ordinary cigarettes."

"I can't imagine Sally getting mixed up in that," Peggy said again, remembering the happy family of that one weekend so long ago. "I can't believe her parents would let her get mixed up in something like that."

Jane shrugged. "All I know is what I heard. I guess

her parents didn't know some of the things she was doing until it was too late."

"You said some of them were suspended. You mean they didn't graduate?"

"Sally's name wasn't on the list of seniors." Then Jane looked at Peggy curiously. "You said she called you? What did she want?"

"She wants me to meet her for lunch. Next Wednesday."

Jane continued to look at her with a slight frown. "I wonder why she called you."

"I'm as much in the dark as you," Peggy answered as Jane started up the stairs. "We hardly know each other, so I don't know what we'll find to talk about."

Jane stopped then and looked down at Peggy. "Just don't get too wrapped up in her problems, will you? If what I hear is true, she's in a group that's different from anything you're used to. She's not a church kid, you know, and isn't about to become one either."

"You think she's a hopeless case?"

"I don't know," Jane answered soberly. "But I don't want you to be too optimistic and then be disappointed."

4

Conversation with Ann

ANN PROPPED THE PILLOW behind her and looked across at Peggy sitting cross-legged on the twin bed near the window.

"I can't believe the summer has gone by so quickly. It seems like such a short time ago that we had that party at your house and I was talking about all the miles I'd be traveling with the trio. And now they've all been traveled."

"Was it fun?"

"Yes and no," Ann answered slowly. "It's kind of hard to be on the go so much and meet new people constantly. You can't get enough sleep when you stay in people's homes and they want to visit after the service is over. It wasn't so bad for me because I just had to play the piano, but when the other girls were tired it showed in their voices. No, I wouldn't say it was fun. But it was an experience I'm glad I had—for a lot of reasons," she finished thoughtfully.

"Will you be glad to get back to school?"

Ann laughed. "That's a loaded question. Am I glad I'll see Bob again soon? Natch."

"Has he written very often?"

"Every day. I didn't *get* a letter every day because we were on the move all the time. But they all caught up with me eventually. It was fun getting a batch of them at one time."

"He had more incentive to write than Bill did. We only got two letters the whole summer. Of course Candy heard more often and passed on news. You know my dad is there this month?"

"Yes, Bob wrote that he had come. Don't tell me he took *that* as his vacation?" Ann laughed at the face Peggy made in reply. "It'll be some vacation if he does all the hard work the two guys have done all summer."

"If I know my father, he'll do it whether he has to or not. Where else do you think Bill got his eager-beaver, going-the-second-mile qualities? But anyway, Dad was expecting it to be a change for him. He said it would give him enough physical exercise to last him for a whole year of sitting and grading English themes."

"Well, that's one way of looking at it," Ann agreed. "Speaking of English themes, when do you have to be back at school?"

"Not until the fifteenth. I can't get too excited about it at this point because it all seems so remote still."

"Maybe you would be if Dan were going there," Ann said slyly.

Peggy nodded calmly. "Probably," and smiled back. Then she looked across at Ann, screwed the cap back on a bottle of fingernail polish she had been using, and said, "I have the feeling you're just killing time waiting to tell me why you really came over here tonight. We could have discussed all these other things by phone, you know."

Ann nodded and looked beyond Peggy through the

window into the night. "I've got so many things running through my mind that I'm having trouble sorting them out even for myself," she said finally, almost as though she were talking to herself. "I've never thought that I was—shallow, I guess is the word I want—but this summer I've done more serious thinking about people and life and Christianity than I've ever done before. I've discovered how sheltered my life has been—is. Even at school all my close friends are right on campus and come from the same background and think the way I do, and believe about God exactly the way I do."

She stopped, still with that faraway look in her dark blue eyes. "But this summer I've met kids who have had a completely different life from mine, and they've made me see things in a different light."

"I thought you were with church kids most of the time. I mean, most of your singing was in churches, wasn't it?"

"Yes, a lot of them are kids who go to church, but church isn't a part of their lives the way it has been for us. It's just another activity they can take or leave alone. And if Christianity doesn't have any real meaning for church kids, how can they be a convincing witness to those who never come to church—the ones you read about in the papers?"

"You mean the kids on drugs?" Peggy asked, thinking of what Jane had hinted about Sally.

"Well, yes, eventually those are the ones I mean. But before they get that far, lots of kids our age are rebellious without knowing just why they are. They're in a sort of vacuum. There isn't any reality or meaning in their lives, and maybe they don't really want any, even though they keep saying they do. There isn't anything that really takes hold of them. You know? Some of them get all excited about projects like—oh, demonstrating for peace or something—but it doesn't go deep enough to make them want to do anything constructive." She looked at Peggy anxiously. "I'm not running them down. They're like this because they don't have any purpose in life."

"It's hard for me to sympathize with that viewpoint," Peggy admitted honestly.

"I know, I'm the same way. Even Bob gets impatient with that kind of an attitude. With all his problems during high school, he was never really in a—a—suspended state—"

Ann stopped, looked at Peggy, and they both howled with laughter.

Finally Ann wiped her eyes and said, "Really though, even though most of his teachers saw to it that he was suspended routinely, he always knew what he wanted out of life. He certainly was never apathetic."

"But I don't see any difference in the way he used to be and these others you're talking about. If kids are unsaved, they're unsaved, and so of course they are going to have problems and be missing something—"

Ann shook her head quickly and positively. "It's not that simple, Peggy, really it isn't. I used to think so too, but I've been with people this summer who have changed my thinking about a lot of things—things I've always taken for granted."

"Like what?" Peggy asked curiously.

Ann took a deep breath. "I used to think that black was black and white was white and that was all there was to anything. All my life everything has always been either/or with me."

"But——"

"Don't worry, I haven't changed what I believe about the Lord. I know that has to be an either/or thing, that you have to believe in Jesus Christ to be saved and have eternal life. There aren't any shades of gray in that for me. But it's—well, I guess it's my *attitude* that's different. I'm not as critical of people who don't look at life the way I do, because I see now that they've been brought up differently from me. At least I'm trying not to be critical."

She stopped then and looked at Peggy pleadingly. "If you don't see what I mean, how can I expect anyone else to?"

But it was Peggy now who was staring out the window, seeing things that weren't there as she said slowly, "I've been remembering Phyllis—" The words hung in the air between them as she turned to look directly at Ann, wondering if she would get the connection.

"That's it!" Ann cried excitedly. "Her eyes! Before she was saved, I mean. Remember how—how—what word do I want? Vacant? No, that's not exactly it—"

"Empty," said Peggy still with that miles-away note.

"That's exactly the impression I've had when I've talked to kids this summer. It's eerie." Ann shivered. "Some people say it's because more kids use drugs now and you can't always tell that they are. But that wasn't Phyllis' trouble. Her whole life was empty and it showed in everything she did. I've found this same emptiness in kids over and over this summer."

Peggy straightened her pillow behind her with a jerk and frowned over at Ann. "Remember how we said we were *always* going to be aware of other people after what we went through with Phyllis? We were *always* going to see other kids' needs and not just stick in our own group all the time? But we didn't. I suppose what you're saying is that there are lots of kids around like Phyllis but we just haven't seen them."

"I guess that's why it hit me so hard this summer and shook me up," Ann replied soberly. She shifted restlessly against the pillow, going on in a rush of words. "One thing I do know is that I've got to get out of the sheltered atmosphere I've been in all my life. I have to find out what other girls my age think. If I don't, how can I ever tell them about the Lord so it will get through to them?"

"Aren't you making a big deal out of nothing, Ann? Say you talk to a girl your age. She's interested in the same things you are—clothes and boys and getting married or getting a job—"

"Yes, but she probably doesn't see them the same way I do because she wasn't raised the same way I was. We might be using the same words but each of us would mean them differently."

"How do you mean?"

"Well, take marriage for instance. I wouldn't think of marrying somone who wasn't a Christian. I wouldn't even have dated Bob before he was saved. That doesn't mean I wouldn't have talked to him or been nice to him, but I wouldn't have dated him seriously. And of course I wouldn't think of living with him before we are married. But here's a girl who doesn't think of marriage as being such a serious step. She gets married, but she figures if it doesn't work out she can always get a divorce and then, if she wants to, she can marry someone else. But there's this other girl who doesn't think you necessarily have to marry the person you fall in love with, so she doesn't. And so she and her boyfriend just live together anyway."

"So?"

"So I talk to either one of them from my viewpoint without understanding theirs and I won't get anywhere with them."

"But what if your viewpoint happens to be right?"

"Sure it's right," Ann agreed. "I know that from the Bible and from all my folks have taught me all my life. But if I don't care enough to find out why they think the way they do—which is what makes them act the way they do—then I'll just not bother with them simply because they don't agree 100 percent with me. And then I've lost any chance of reaching them for the Lord. See what I mean?"

Peggy looked across at her friend, impressed by the intensity with which Ann, usually so placid and calm, was speaking.

"Yes, I guess I do," she said finally.

"Bob and I talked about this a lot last year. We were helping in a youth group in a church near school, and I found that my years of growing up in a minister's family had really built a wall around me. Oh, don't get me wrong, Peggy. I'm glad for the wall and its protection. But I'd like to give other kids the same kind of protection."

"How can you if they don't have the same kind of experiences?"

"I think we all have pretty much the same problems no matter where we live or how we're brought up. Most of us have the same needs. And of course the most important one is to have our sins forgiven by believing in Christ. But because we grew up differently, we react differently to the gospel message. This is what I'm groping around trying to explain even though it isn't too clear in my own mind. Look, Peg, I know everybody doesn't believe the Bible is the Word of God the way I do. This is something I just accepted from the time I was a little child, and I don't think I'm gullible just because I believe what my parents told me to. I never had any reason to doubt their word about it. But someone else—Bob, for example—didn't have this teaching all his life and he had to have it proved to him. But I can't get all shook and blame him or criticize him because he doesn't believe as easily as I do."

"You really think this is important, don't you? This seeing the other person's viewpoint."

"Yes, I do. And Bob's experiences this summer have made me feel surer than ever. His folks are rich, you know, so they have always given him everything he wanted, especially when they were trying to get him straightened out before he was saved. He's never known what it is to want something and not be able to have it. And, of course, ordinary necessities like clothes he just took for granted. But now all summer he's been with these kids who have so little at the orphanage. You'd never believe how poor some of them are. Some kids didn't go to school because they didn't have decent clothes to wear. Others took turns going, one brother one day and another the next so they could share the pants and shoes. So naturally Bob feels out of it with them. He can't understand why having things, just *having* them, is so important to these kids."

"But he and Bill agreed before they went that they wouldn't even take their best clothes along—" Peggy began but Ann interrupted impatiently.

"That's not the point! The thing is, they've got them when they want them. Look, Bob's got a pair of beat-up shoes that he wears a lot just because they're comfortable. He's got eight or so other pairs, but he likes these. And it's just because he's got the good ones that he can wear the old ones. See?"

Peggy nodded but said, "In one of Bill's letters he raved about how crazy the boys were over Bob."

"Oh, sure. He can goof around with them and they think he's terrific. But when it comes to talking seriously with them, he freezes because he's scared he won't get through to them. Of course, the thing that helps is that he really wants to be a friend, and I guess the kids can feel that."

"So what is all this leading up to?" Peggy asked. "There must be some reason why you are so steamed up over this right now."

Ann nodded. "I've decided to work a little bit with this club Lisa has that I mentioned to you. Instead of going home, I'm going to stay at the Vanaceks the next couple of weeks. Lisa was especially anxious for it to go on at least until school starts."

"Do you think they'll come for you?"

"I don't know."

"How many usually come?"

"Lisa said sometimes three and sometimes fifteen. It depends on what else is going on and how the girls feel on that particular day. She never pressures them at all."

"To me the most miraculous part is that Mrs. Van-

acek lets them come, now especially when Lisa won't
be there," Peggy exclaimed. "What are you going to
do with them?"

"Lisa said anything I want to. She doesn't have a
Bible study of any kind. I guess most of the girls
wouldn't know a Bible if they saw one. They sing and
talk and have sewing and cooking lessons of sorts.
Nothing formal at all. But as I told you before, Lisa
gets in the salvation story every time in some way or
other. She's really terrific at it, Peg. You wouldn't believe the in she has with these girls."

"It's quite a job you've taken on."

"Don't I know it!" Ann agreed fervently. "Mrs. Vanacek is going to help by giving a couple of lessons on
some of her Hungarian recipes." She looked at Peggy
and said hopefully, "I thought maybe you could come
once and show them something about designing. You
know, just the bare essentials of which colors look good
together and which ones don't."

"Do you think they'd be interested?"

"Who isn't interested in clothes?" Ann retorted.

Peggy was silent, thinking of the neighborhood Ann
would be living in. Of course, Lisa had lived there all
her life, but she belonged and Ann was an outsider.
And besides that, there would be Lisa's drunken father
stumbling around.

"Why not stay here?" she suggested. "We've got
plenty of room and it would be fun having you. We
could work out something about your transportation
back and forth."

"Thanks, but I can't," Ann answered. "This would
be too much like home. I'd end up spending most of
the time here, and I wouldn't get the feel of the girls'

lives. Lisa worked and could only be with them in the evening, but I want to be with them during the day too and go swimming and things. Besides, I wouldn't want to hurt Mrs. Vanacek's feelings. She has Lisa's room all ready for me, and I don't want her to think it isn't good enough for me. After all, she can see the difference between this house and hers."

Then she looked over at Peggy and laughed. "Don't look like a worried mother hen. I'll be all right."

5

A Changed Sally

PEGGY WENT INTO TOWN with Miss Murphy early Wednesday to have time to shop at Groton's before meeting Sally. She had promised her mother she would look for a thank you gift for Aunt Emily, although neither of them knew exactly what they wanted. She spent so much time looking without finding anything that was just right, that she had to hurry to get down to the first floor perfume counter where she and Sally had agreed to meet. As she came down the escalator from the gift shop on the fifth floor, she looked across the crowds below, standing on tiptoe to see the perfume counter. There were only a few people there, several fiftyish matrons, a thin girl in tight slacks and a baggy sweater, and a short, round man looking out of place in that spot. No one was there who could be Sally.

And then the girl in slacks and sweater turned to face the escalator, and Peggy stared. It was Sally, but not the round-faced, well-scrubbed girl Peggy had been looking for. She stood for a moment at the foot of the escalator, searching for the word to describe her. Haggard? Certainly that, for Sally was so thin she was almost gaunt. But it was more than that.

She worked her way through the aisles past other

shoppers and came up behind Sally, who was leaning against the counter while a clerk hovered nearby watching her suspiciously.

"Sally?" she asked doubtfully.

The girl turned and looked at Peggy, and then a smile brought back a faint reminder of the Sally of eighth grade.

"Hi," Peggy said nervously, not comfortable under the stare of this stranger who looked her up and down.

"You said you hadn't changed," Sally finally said accusingly. "But you have. You used to be kind of a scared bunny, and now you're not. You've got—self-confidence. It sticks out all over you. What'd you do? Inherit a million?"

"It's just your imagination," Peggy protested, sure that Sally was joking. "I haven't changed a bit."

"You have to me." Sally kept staring at her intently. Then abruptly she added, "I'll bet you think I have too."

Peggy's mind raced frantically, trying to think of what to say without telling Sally what she really thought of her limp tangled hair with the dark roots that showed so plainly, the smeared mascara and the white lipstick that caked her lips. The matching white nail polish was chipped and didn't cover the dirt under her fingernails, and Peggy could hardly keep back a shudder. She finally said, "Well, I must admit I'd never have recognized you as a blonde if you hadn't prepared me. And you are a lot thinner."

The clerk had moved closer to them now and she said to Peggy, "May I help you?" but she kept on watching Sally, who laughed harshly.

"She's had her eye on me for the last twenty minutes.

You don't suppose she thinks I'm a suspicious-looking character, do you?" Then she grabbed Peggy's arm. "Come on, let's find a place to eat. I'm starved."

They pushed through the revolving door, elbowing their way through the crowds. Out on the street Sally stopped and looked at Peggy again.

"Maybe you don't want to eat with me after all. As you can see, I didn't take time to dress to the teeth. It's too much bother."

Peggy would have liked to tell her that she might at least have combed her hair, but she didn't. Instead she said, "I can stand the way you look." Then almost involuntarily she added, "If you can."

Sally had started walking again at Peggy's first words but stopped abruptly as she heard the end of the sentence. "There! That's what I mean," she exclaimed. "When I knew you before, you wouldn't have said that. You *have* changed."

Peggy had regretted the words the minute they were out, afraid Sally would be offended and leave her on the spot. But having said them, she couldn't take them back, so she smiled at Sally and said, "Just a joke." Then as Sally started on again without saying anything or smiling back, Peggy hurried to keep up, wondering what they would talk about through a whole lunch hour with only the memories to share of one school year so long ago. It wouldn't have been difficult with the Sally she remembered but this one was a complete stranger.

She followed Sally into a pizza place and to a booth. After they had ordered, Sally opened her shoulder purse and took out a crumpled pack of cigarettes. She offered it to Peggy, who shook her head.

"No, thanks."

"It's OK," Sally said, still holding out the pack. "They're straight."

"No, thanks," Peggy said again.

Sally took one and returned the pack to her purse. Then she asked, "Is that all you're going to say?" She seemed disappointed and Peggy looked at her in surprise. "You asked and I answered."

Sally lit her cigarette, blew a cloud of smoke and looked at Peggy through it. "I suppose you're too righteous to smoke."

The words could have been insulting except that they were said so matter-of-factly that there wasn't any personal sting to them. Peggy replied, "I guess I've just never thought about smoking because nobody does in the crowd I go with. I've honestly never been offered a cigarette before."

"You should try one."

"Why? I'm not about to ruin my health."

Sally gestured derisively. "I've heard all the cancer percentages. But, so what? You can't run half scared all your life. You can get killed walking across the street on the green light. Anyway, I really don't smoke that much." She ground out the partially smoked cigarette and looked across at Peggy with a funny expression on her face as she said, "I guess I did it just now to get your reaction."

"Was it what you expected?" Peggy asked curiously.

"Frankly, no. Of course, I don't know you very well, but I thought you'd get all fired up over my offer and preach me a sermon on the evils of smoking."

"What made you think I'd do that?"

Sally waited while the waitress served them and

then said, "The thing I remember about you from way back is that you were pretty religious, and I wondered if you still were. Are you?"

Instead of answering, Peggy asked, "Is that all you remember about me?"

Sally shrugged. "That's the main thing. That and how mousy you were. You never did speak up for yourself. But since you've changed in that way, I thought you might have in the other. So I thought I'd find out." She was ladling sugar in her coffee as she spoke and didn't look up, so Peggy couldn't tell if she really wanted to know or was just making idle conversation.

She stirred her own coffee thoughtfully before she answered. "I haven't changed in either way really. In fact, it's really funny to have you think that the worm has turned. Thanks. I'll remember this for the future. As for what I believe, I can tell you positively that I haven't changed that. I remember your asking me what it meant to be a Christian. I told you then it was accepting the Lord Jesus as your Saviour and that it was the most important thing you could ever do in all your life. I still believe that."

"You had to get your sermon in, didn't you?" Sally asked mockingly. "Tell me, what do you remember about me?"

Peggy answered immediately, "Your family and the fun you all had together." Then she added thoughtfully, "I guess that impressed me most because I was away from home and was pretty lonely sometimes, even though my relatives were nice enough. You were all so close to each other."

She looked across at Sally, who was slumped in one

corner of the booth, her tangled mass of hair falling across her cheeks and over her shoulders. Her remembrance of Sally was that her face showed everything she was thinking. But that wasn't so now when she finally lifted her head and stared back at Peggy with absolutely no expression on her face, not even interest in what they had been talking about. Peggy had the sudden horrible thought that she was making a big mistake in talking to Sally about her family. Maybe something terrible had happened to them all that made Sally act like this about them. But surely Jane or Mrs. Tremont would have said something to warn her so she wouldn't blunder in.

She decided it was better to find out and asked hesitantly, "How are your folks?"

"OK." The brief answer closed off any further discussion and they finished eating in silence.

Finally Peggy asked, "Where are you working?"

Sally made a face. "I'm waitressing. Temporarily. At a hamburger joint down the street."

"Temporarily?"

"Uh-huh."

"You mean you're looking for another job?"

"No, I mean I'm working just long enough to get enough money so I can quit and loaf until the money runs out. And then I'll have to look for another job— since my folks refuse to support me." The words were almost an afterthought and yet, oddly enough, it seemed to Peggy that she said them deliberately to give information she didn't want to say directly.

Because she didn't know what to say in answer, what polite questions to ask, Peggy was silent. She couldn't help remembering how hard she had worked the past year and the long hours she had put in at the store to have money for school.

Sally watched her with amusement. "You wouldn't do it that way, huh?"

"No."

Peggy couldn't help the flat, positive, almost angry way the word came out, nor the way it jarred in the air between them.

"Why not? What's so bad about taking life easy?"

"I guess money has been too hard to come by in our family—"

"With an aunt and uncle as rich as yours?" Sally jeered.

"Their money isn't ours," Peggy flashed back.

Sally gave her usual shrug. "Sorry. Any other reason you don't believe in the easy life?"

Peggy started to answer and then stopped, warned by the note of challenge in Sally's voice as though she were baiting her into an argument. And the last thing she wanted was to get into an argument with her at their first meeting and maybe not have another chance to see her. So she said as casually as possible, "Oh, I guess I just like doing things in the conventional way."

"That's not much of an answer."

"It satisfies me," Peggy answered, still determined not to get involved in a big discussion.

"Why do you want to stay in the same old rut? Do things just because it's expected of you? Believe all this stuff about God because someone told you to? Don't you know the old morals are out? Nobody believes them anymore. The future belongs to us and we have to change it to suit ourselves."

Peggy was silent, thinking of the times she'd heard about kids who had this philosophy and how she'd always supposed they got their ideas and values twisted because of a rotten homelife. But Sally? What could she blame her mixed-up ideas on? Certainly not on her childhood. She wondered too how many times Sally had heard and repeated these words. They sounded too well rehearsed to be spontaneous.

Without changing her flat, almost disinterested tone of voice, Sally went on. "Everybody should have a chance to live his own life and not be tied down by family rules that are out of date. Since my family didn't agree with my ideas, I moved out so I could live the way I want to."

"I suppose that's one way to do it. Me? I have it too easy at home and like my family too much to move out," Peggy retorted. Then she looked at Sally's thin face and shadowed eyes; her throat was suddenly tight with choked tears. She was being cowardly to let this moment slip by without showing Sally the other side of life. So she said, "Besides, I don't think it's the right way to live. Sure it's OK to be on your own, but you don't have to throw away all your convictions and beliefs. That's no way for anyone to live. God didn't intend for anyone to live without Him."

This time Sally's head jerked up and she stared at Peggy belligerently.

"That's your real reason, isn't it? You think the whole world is supposed to live by rules God made up."

"Yes, don't you?"

"No! I don't believe in God."

"Why not?"

"Well, look at the mess everything is in. War, sick

eople all over, poverty, cruelty, crime—how can you
e dumb enough to believe in a God who lets every-
hing get into such a mess?"

Peggy shoved her plate away from her in exaspera-
ion. "Honestly, Sally, that's such a worn-out excuse.
You really ought to come up with a better one than that
f you're going to make one up at all. How can *you* be
dumb enough to blame the world's mess on God?"

"Who else is there to blame?"

"Us. People. I'm not saying I've got all the answers,
but I do know the world wasn't a mess when God made
t."

Sally stared back for a moment and then shrugged,
her brief show of interest lost. "Oh, well, who cares?
It's too much trouble to figure it out. Nobody can be
sure of anything anyway. Tell me about yourself. How
long will you be here?"

This sudden shifting of interest was hard to get used
to, but Peggy decided to go along with it and talk about
any subject Sally wanted to. She had to be careful not
to lecture or preach at her. She replied, "Oh, ten days
or so. Then I'll be home for a couple of weeks before
school starts." She had said all this on the phone but
either Sally didn't remember or was just making conversation.

Now Sally said mockingly, "College, huh? The usual
nice little middle-class pattern."

Peggy found it impossible to get mad at her, because
even though the words were meant to be sneering and
nasty, they didn't come out that way. Struck again by
how flat and tired Sally sounded, she said impulsively,
"You don't really believe all this, do you?"

Sally stared back defiantly. "Well, isn't it true? Aren'
you living just the way you're expected to?"

"Sure, but so what? It also happens to be the wa
I want to live."

"I should think you'd want to break away from i
all and be your own boss."

"Well, I am as much as I want to be—"

But Sally had lost interest again and yawned. "I'n
sorry, Peggy, I'm not good company today. I was uj
late last night and I'm dead." She stood up. "It was
nice seeing you. I don't go along with anything you've
said, but I'm—I'm glad you haven't changed toc
much."

"Can't we meet again before I leave? Come out to
my aunt's house and let me repay the slumber party."

Sally's laugh was harsh. "I don't even go to see my
own family, so why should I bother seeing yours?"

"Then let's have lunch again. Or let me come and
visit you."

Sally looked at her oddly for a moment and then
shook her head. "You still don't get the picture, do
you? I don't live where I used to. And you won't like
where I live now, or the way I live, or the people I
live with."

Peggy leaned across the table and looked up at her.
"Look, Sally, this may not mean anything to you, but
you were a friend to me a long time ago when I needed
a friend. You didn't do much maybe, but I've always
remembered you. Friends aren't friends just because of
where they live or the way they live. I think you need
a friend now and I'd like to be it as long as I'm here."

"I've got lots of friends," Sally replied sulkily.

"You can use another one, can't you?"

Sally looked at her. "You really want to visit me?"

"If you'll let me." Peggy looked at her watch. "I've got to meet Miss Murphy in about an hour. Is that time enough?"

Sally didn't answer but stood looking down at her through narrowed eyes. Then she asked abruptly, "My folks haven't called you, have they?" Before Peggy could answer, she said, "No—no, I guess they wouldn't know about you. They've snooped around all my other friends." She thought a moment. "If I take you to my apartment, you've got to promise you won't call my parents and tell them where I'm living. My mother gets these soft, sentimental moments and she'd be sure to come crying around and try to get me to go back."

"I won't call them," Peggy promised.

It was easy to promise almost anything because the whole thing seemed so unreal. Walking along the sidewalk beside Sally and then getting on a bus for what seemed like an interminable ride was unreal also. Peggy told herself over and over again that this sullen, nervous, dirty girl couldn't be Sally, and yet she was. She couldn't be living by choice in the dirt-littered neighborhood where they got off the bus, and yet she was. She couldn't possibly have chosen to live in the wretched tenement building she led Peggy into, and yet she had.

The odors in the dimly lighted hallway were so strong that Peggy felt her stomach turn over. She held her breath as long as she could and then took a brief gulp of air that only made her feel sick. They walked up the first flight of sagging steps, with Peggy nervously wondering how far up they had to go. At the top of the second landing, Sally turned to her. "Wait here a minute," she said, and went up the next flight, knocked twice on a door, opened it and looked in and then turned and leaned over the railing.

"OK, come on up."

Peggy took another cautious breath and held it while she hurried up the stairs, stepped into the room and look nervously around. She realized that she had dreaded meeting any of Sally's friends and was weak with relief when she found there was no one else there.

It was then that the condition of the room struck her like a physical blow. It wasn't a home; it was just a place to stay to keep one off the street. She stared around the cluttered room in horrified disbelief. She saw the remnants of several meals on the bare table, the unmade beds in the next room, watched in horror as several cockroaches scurried up the side of the kitchen cabinet and disappeared into the stack of greasy dishes in the dirty sink. Her stomach turned over again and she wondered wildly what she would do if her lunch actually started to come up.

And all the time her mind was asking how Sally could have left the clean world she had grown up in for this—this hole. Or, having left it for what she might have mistakenly thought would be a glamorous life, how could she continue to live in this filth? It wasn't the cheapness of the rickety furnishings nor even the absence of rugs and pictures and lamps; it was the odor and the squalor and the obvious not caring that were so appalling.

She was aware then that Sally was looking at her with a mocking smile on her lips as she followed her eyes around the room. "Different from the last time you visited me, isn't it?"

"Yes, it is." Peggy tried to answer calmly, but then she couldn't hold back the cry, "Why, Sally? Why do you want to live like this?" and she threw out her arm to take it all in.

Sally turned abruptly and walked over to stare out the dirt-streaked window, pushing aside limp, ragged curtains. She had taken off her bulky sweater and tossed it on a pile of other clothes on a kitchen chair. Peggy felt her throat ache with the effort it took to hold back tears as she saw Sally's bony shoulders underneath a sheer nylon blouse and saw the nervous gesture of her thin hands as she lit another cigarette.

She turned then to face Peggy. "Let's just say that I like this kind of life. I can do what I want when I want with no one to boss me around."

"I can't believe it." Peggy looked at the sink and then away quickly.

Sally raised and lowered her shoulders in her familiar shrug and leaned back against the wall by the window. "Well, naturally, I'd rather have four-inch-thick carpeting on the floors and an automatic dishwasher and a color TV, but those things I can't afford. This I can— even if it doesn't meet with the approval of my former friends."

"You had the carpeted floors at home—"

Sally cut her off with a blazing, "OK, if you want to know, I live here because my folks kicked me out. They didn't want me around soiling their carpeted floors!"

"I sound like a broken record maybe, but I don't believe that either."

"Well, it's true. They told me to get out and stay out until I could dress the way they wanted me to and

act the way they wanted me to. I was glad to get out.
I was sick of their bossing," she finished sullenly.

"What's wrong with their wanting you to be clean
and decently dressed?" Peggy demanded as she looked
at Sally's tangled hair and dirty nails and soiled slacks.
She didn't dare look at the sink and its contents again.
"That's one of the things I most remember about your
family. Everything was so clean and cheerful and
warm."

But Sally interrupted sulkily, "It wasn't just my
clothes and cigarettes. They claimed I was a bad influence on—"

She stopped short and the muscles along the line of
her cheek contracted as she bit her lip.

Peggy finished the sentence for her deliberately and
challengingly, "On the monsters?"

Sally just stared down at the floor without answering
as Peggy went on, "I've told you that I remember how
affectionately you used to call them that and how much
they loved it."

She was sure this memory hurt Sally more than anything else could, and she prayed she was doing the
right thing in using it deliberately to hurt her more.
"Remember what I said about how impressed I was
with your family and how much I envied you because
you all had such a good time together and your parents
and sisters were so close—"

"Stop it!" Sally shouted, putting her hands over her
ears and turning away to lean her forehead against the
wall.

And Peggy felt herself relaxing as a faint hope began
to warm her. If these memories could bother Sally,

perhaps she wasn't too far gone to reach if there were just enough time.

"I'm sorry," she said quietly. "I didn't mean to hurt you. And I suppose you find it hard to believe that I want to be your friend. But I have to try to help you." She waited but Sally didn't move or make a sound.

Finally Peggy said, "I have to go now, but please let me see you again before I go back home. Please?"

"Well, you know where I live," was the muffled reply. Then as Peggy opened the door and looked nervously out into the hall, Sally jerked around. "Wait a minute. I'll take you back to the store. You might get lost in this jungle. I've been."

And Peggy, waiting while Sally pulled on her sweater, thought, *And you still are.*

She followed Sally down the stairs and to the bus, thankful that she could meet Miss Murphy and go back to her familiar, secure world.

6

Some Detective Work

PEGGY DIALED the Vanacek number as soon as she got home. When Anton answered, she asked for Ann.

"I've got a candidate for your club or meeting or whatever," she began without preliminary greetings.

"Good. Who?"

"Did I ever mention Sally to you from when I lived out here before?"

"I don't think so—"

"Probably not, because I hadn't gotten to know her very well and she wouldn't have meant anything to you. Well, I've just come from talking to her and is she ever in a mess."

She filled Ann in on the details and then waited for her reaction. Ann didn't answer for a moment and then she said hesitantly, "The only problem is, she's older than most of the girls who come."

"I didn't know there was an age limit."

"There isn't exactly. It's just that none of those who come are through school; I mean, through because they've graduated. The ones who don't go are dropouts."

"Well, Sally isn't exactly crazy about school either, if that's any help," Peggy retorted. "She's finished because she was expelled last year when she was a senior."

But Ann went on slowly, "Another thing, none of these girls is from a nice home that they just up and left because they wanted to. They all come from pretty horrible situations that they can't leave. Most of them would like to but they don't have any place to go and no money."

"Yes, but Sally isn't getting any help from her family. She has a job, or sort of one, and she lives in a really terrible place," Peggy argued, not understanding why Ann was so reluctant to let Sally come.

"But, you see, she *has* had it nice, and I'm afraid the other girls will be able to tell just from the way she looks and talks. I'm wondering if she will fit in——"

"Believe me, when you see her, you'd never believe what a nice home she comes from or how she used to look. I can still smell where she lives now. I'm sorry if that sounds snobbish, but it makes me mad because she lives in such an awful place when she doesn't have to." Then to Ann's continued silence, she added simply, "All I know is that she needs help and I don't know where else to go for it."

"I guess that's the answer then," Ann replied. "Do you think she'll come if you invite her?"

"I don't know. I wanted to clear it with you first and actually I'm going to be afraid to ask her because she's anti-everything. But there's something else that's worrying me now that we're talking this way. You talk about Sally not being accepted. Will *I* fit in? I'm more of an outsider to these girls than Sally will be."

"As long as you're Lisa's friend, you're in. About eight came over last night and just fooled around talking. They looked at me pretty suspiciously, but since I'm Lisa's friend I get by."

"We can't pass Sally off that way though," Peggy warned. "She doesn't know Lisa and she'll probably say so. If she does come, it would spoil everything— any chance of reaching her if she got antagonized by someone—"

"It's possible that she's the one who will antagonize everybody else," Ann broke in.

"Um, you're right. Well, all we can do is try. What time is it Friday? . . . Eight? OK, see you then."

Peggy hung up the phone and turned as Jane said from the doorway, "I'm afraid you're wasting your time if you're trying to reform Sally."

"You know it isn't reforming she needs," Peggy answered and then asked, "Just what is the trouble with her and her family? You only told me a little bit."

"I don't really know much more. I heard that she got started with the wrong bunch of kids when she was a sophomore. Her folks didn't know anything about it and when they found out they were really mad about it. Then to get even or something, she started dating a fellow who had dropped out of school. She started smoking and things just sort of snowballed on her. Her parents told her she either had to straighten up or move out—"

"That's what she said, only her story is that it was all one-sided and that her parents just made her get out, period."

"I suppose they were afraid of her influence on her sisters. I don't know where she went."

"It's a horrible place," Peggy said, seeing the filth again and shuddering.

"Probably not—" Jane began. She stopped and looked at Peggy. "How do you know?"

"I was there with her this afternoon after we had lunch. We took a long bus ride. It's someplace on Ninth Avenue and Twenty-fourth Street, I think the sign said."

"But that's a terrible neighborhood! Anybody who reads the newspapers knows that."

"The neighborhood fits the building she lives in. I thought I'd lose my lunch just over the smells in the hall."

"Oh, you dope! The smells are the least part of it. It's dangerous just to be there."

"I didn't think of that part of it," Peggy admitted. "All I thought about was keeping in touch with her and getting her to trust me. I didn't even watch where we were going. Of course I never dreamed she would live in a place like that when I remembered what her home was like—*is* like. Why does her family let her live that way?"

"How can they keep her from it? If she's moved out, she's moved out. If she didn't live by their standards when she was home, she sure isn't going to when she's on her own. Just be careful," Jane pleaded. "Don't go there with her alone again."

After Jane left, Peggy still sat, thinking of the difference in families. It was funny how those you thought had every chance of turning out well sometimes didn't and those you thought would never make it, did. Take theirs, for example. There wasn't one logical reason why their family should have stuck together through so many hard years. There were so many things working against them. Moving frequently, so little money,

their mother's bitterness against life—and often at their
father—the near break when she and Bill had to move
in with relatives for a year and, most important of all,
not having any sure anchor in Christ for so many
years. Any one of these could have destroyed them.
And Sally's family had seemed to her so secure finan-
cially and emotionally even though they were not Christians.

Of course it was Christ who had made the difference
and given them stability. But the fact that the Sanders
were not Christians didn't completely answer the question of what had gone wrong with Sally. Lots of people
who weren't Christians lived normal, ordinary, even
happy lives without going haywire the way Sally had.

There was some nagging memory in her mind about
Sally and her family. Something about their having
gone to church. Someone had written her a letter, she
was sure. Perhaps it was Mrs. Tremont. Peggy reached
for the phone book and ran her finger down the col-
umn for the number. When Mrs. Tremont answered,
she asked the questions that were bothering her.

"Peggy, this is a case that is hard to understand. It's
made me realize how important it is to be sure a person really trusts Christ for salvation and doesn't do
something as an emotional reaction. I thought Sally had
been saved after a talk we had. She and her family suddenly began coming to church. But they only came
three times and then stopped. They didn't get to know
anyone before they lost all interest. And then Sally
seemed to fall apart in high school."

"What about her sisters? What are they like?"

"I've only had one of them and she's a dear. How-
ever, I haven't been able to really talk to her."

"I wish you could. It was the things you talked to me about outside of class that helped me the most."

"Maybe she's sensitive because I asked her about Sally once and she didn't want to talk about her. I've chatted with the parents at PTA and her mother, especially, is charming. I can't believe they drove Sally away."

"But that's what Sally thinks—or at least says she thinks."

"That's more convenient than blaming herself. There's undoubtedly fault on both sides. Sally can't shove it all off on her parents nor they on her."

"I-I have such a helpless feeling about the whole thing. I don't even know how to talk to her."

"Just one word of advice, Peggy, if I may. Since you're going to be here such a short time, don't expect a miracle to happen."

"Shouldn't I?"

There was silence and then Mrs. Tremont answered, "Yes, you're right, Peggy, you should expect a miracle. I guess what I really meant was that that's exactly what it will take to get through to Sally. And it might not happen easily or quickly."

"Well, naturally, I don't expect to do anything myself. I don't know if you know anything about Lisa's club?"

"Yes, but—" Mrs. Tremont hesitated and then went on reluctantly, "But I'm not sure that's the answer in this case. These girls have such absolutely different backgrounds from Sally—"

"I know. Ann told me some of the case histories."

"You have to see them to believe it," Mrs. Tremont warned. "And believing is easier than understanding how people can survive in the conditions some of those girls grow up in. I really see red when people talk about how they should be able to lift themselves out of a bad home situation. It's just not that easy. Some do, like Lisa, but some don't—and can't."

"Maybe if Sally sees them it will bring her to her senses and make her want to get out of the mess she's in." But Peggy stopped abruptly at the memory of Sally's apartment. "No," she said ruefully. "Living conditions don't mean that much to her, not if you look at the wretched place she's in right now. And that's one of the hardest things for me to understand about this whole business with Sally. I mean, how she can leave her home and all its comforts and live in the filth she's in now? She grew up being clean. How can she get used to being dirty? I know I sound like a broken record on this, but that's what bothers me most about it all."

"Apparently it's part of the whole pattern of whatever she's rebelling against. And I think you'll have to remember this when you talk to her about becoming a Christian. Telling her how much better her life will be if she accepts Christ won't reach her if she doesn't care what condition her life is in. You may have to find some other way to get through to her."

"Um, I hadn't thought of that," Peggy replied. Bits of her conversation with Ann went through her mind. This was just what Ann had said about the importance of seeing the other person's viewpoint. Even if her own were right, she couldn't force it on Sally. She frowned at the enormity of the problem as she said slowly, "I'm scared about this whole thing. Since I don't know what to say to Sally, I find myself getting mad at her instead of being sympathetic because she's in a mess she doesn't have to be in."

"Does she resent it when you get mad?"

"No, that's a surprising thing. She seems to admire me for not being what she calls mousy—the way she said I used to be. And she says she remembers that I was religious. The thing I get mad at is not her but the fact that there's no reason for what she's doing."

"There's some reason for it, Peggy, even though you don't see it. So don't just brush her actions off as silly or unreasonable. The fact that she called you must mean that she wants help of some kind from someone. Maybe you can get something across to her that someone else will be able to work on later."

"I know. When I think of how little time I have with her I have to remember the Bible's 'one plants and another waters' idea."

"But it's only God who gives the results," Mrs. Tremont added. "In a case that looks as hopeless as this one, it's a help to remember that God can do the impossible."

" 'God specializes in things thought impossible, and He can do what no other one can do' " Peggy quoted softly. "Thanks, Mrs. Tremont, thanks a lot. I'll let you know what happens."

Jane stuck her head in the door just then. "How about playing me a game of ping-pong after lunch?"

"OK, but I won't be much competition. With Bill gone all summer I'm out of practice."

After winning four games straight, Jane stopped and looked at her accusingly. "Are you just purposely letting me win?"

"I told you I wasn't very good," Peggy reminded

her. "I could use the excuse that I keep thinking about Sally, but that would only be part of the reason you beat me. The biggest part is that you're better than I am."

"You've really got yourself in a bind over her, haven't you?"

Peggy nodded. "My problem right now is that I want to invite her to the meeting at Lisa's on Friday and I haven't any idea how to get hold of her. I never thought to ask for her phone number and there's nothing listed under Sanders in that part of town. Her folks are listed but they don't know where she's living. And anyway, I promised not to call them."

"Do you know where she works?"

"She's a waitress someplace, but I didn't even think to ask where—wait a minute. What did she say? Something about a hamburger joint down the street."

"Where? I mean where were you when she said that?"

"At some pizza place."

"That's a help."

"Well, we were someplace near Groton's. It only took about five minutes to walk there." She looked at Jane hopefully. "Are you thinking we might be able to find it?"

"It won't hurt to try. Are you sure she'll be working tomorrow?"

"Probably. Today was her day off."

"I know Miss Murphy is going to town tomorrow morning about ten. Let's ask if we can go with her and maybe we can bum around on our own and find this place."

When Miss Murphy had dropped them off at the

department store, agreeing to pick them up at two o'clock, Jane said, "OK, private eye, which way now?"

Peggy looked around. "Well, we came out that door and walked this way."

Jane followed as she started off, trying to see landmarks that she hadn't paid any attention to the day before. After walking a couple of blocks she said triumphantly, "This is it. I remember the sign. And the slogan in the window."

"Great. Now all we have to do is look for a hamburger place. Did she give you any idea how far it was or what direction it might be in? Or even if it was anywhere around here at all?"

"Well, we were sitting in the booth over by the wall. See it?" Jane nodded. "Sally sort of jerked her head backward—you know how you do when you just give a general direction and then she said, 'down the street.' So I suppose it would be in this general area."

"If she was facing that direction and jerked her head this way, the logical place to start looking is farther down this street."

Peggy looked down the street and then back at Jane and shook her head helplessly. "This is probably the most ridiculously foolish thing we could possibly do."

"Except for one thing." Jane's voice was gruff and she cleared her throat before she said, "Before we start, we could ask the Lord to help us. After all, Sally is important to Him too. If we're supposed to find her, won't He take us to the right place?"

Peggy nodded, looking back at Jane wordlessly, unable to say anything out loud because of a confusion of emotions. There was shame that she had so quickly forgotten her words to Mrs. Tremont that only God could do the impossible and thankfulness that Jane saw the importance of prayer. So turning their backs on the people going by and staring in at the window display of imitation pizzas, they asked God to lead them to the right place.

As they started walking, Peggy said, "I think we can omit all the restaurants and concentrate on the strictly hamburger spots."

Four blocks later she clutched Jane's arm. "There! See? There she is. Behind that counter."

Jane looked doubtful. "Are you sure? She doesn't look the same—"

"It is though. Let's go in. It's almost one o'clock and the place doesn't look busy now. Maybe she'll eat with us."

"You go in. I'll eat someplace else and meet you at the store."

"How come?"

"You'll have a better chance to talk to her if you're alone. She might clam up if I'm along. Don't you think?" she finished uncertainly.

"Maybe you're right. OK, I'll see you later then. And, Jane, pray that I'll say the right things. I'm so afraid she'll get mad. She's so touchy about every little thing."

She waited until Jane was out of sight and then opened the door and went up to the counter. "Hi, Sally."

She whirled around. "What are *you* doing here?"

"I came in for lunch. Can you eat with me?"

"I don't want to."

"Please? I hate to eat by myself."

Sally stared at her in anger and then looked around

at the clock behind her. "OK," she said shortly. "But not here. I wouldn't eat in this place if I were starving."

She took off her apron, grabbed her purse and said, "Come on."

When they had each ordered a hamburger in a restaurant two doors down the street, Sally leaned back, lit a cigarette and stared across at Peggy. "OK, I've only got a half hour so say what's on your mind this time."

Peggy plunged in. "I want you to go to a meeting with me Friday—"

"Not a chance!"

"Wait a minute. You don't even know what kind it is."

"With you it will be a religious meeting. Don't try to reform me," she snapped. "I won't stand for it. I like my life the way it is, and I won't have you or anyone else messing it up."

Peggy choked back a scornful laugh at the thought of her life being messed up any more than it was and made herself say calmly, "I just thought you'd like to go with me. I'm not inviting you to a prayer meeting."

"You knew I wouldn't go if you did. And I'll bet that's what this will turn out to be. All I want is for you to leave me alone."

Peggy looked back at her thoughtfully. Since Sally seemed to admire her new frankness, she decided to use it now. Picking her words carefully, she said, "I don't believe that."

"So?"

"You know why I don't?" Peggy persisted.

"I don't care why," Sally answered sullenly. Then,

after several jerky puffs on her cigarette, she ground it out in her empty coffee cup and asked, "Why?"

"Because you were the one who called me in the first place."

"What's that got to do with it?"

"I don't think you would have if you really wanted to be left alone."

"Well, let's just say I'm sorry I called and let it go at that," Sally snapped back crossly.

"You called me and admitted yourself that you mostly remembered me because I was religious. So I think that means you're more interested than you'll let yourself admit," Peggy pursued relentlessly.

Sally didn't answer as she tapped her fingers on the table waiting for the check to come. Peggy looked at her stringy, unkempt hair and her thin cheeks and the green eye shadow she hadn't bothered to put on carefully; she was torn between pity and impatience.

But she repeated evenly, "Since you called me and I think you need help, I don't intend to give up on you until—" She stopped abruptly, not sure how to express all the longing that filled her for Sally.

"Until what?"

"Until you turn back into the happy-go-lucky, clean Sally you used to be."

The words surprised her because she hadn't intended to be quite so emphatic about the clean angle. She could see that Sally was surprised too.

And then Sally said unexpectedly and mockingly, "Oh, yeah, I know all about the 'cleanliness is next to godliness' bit. That's a nice little proverb my grandmother likes to quote."

"Yes, I think being clean is part of being a Christian." Peggy impulsively pulled her New Testament out of her purse, thumbed to the verse she wanted and read, "Be not deceived: neither fornicators, nor idolaters . . . nor thieves . . . nor drunkards, nor revilers, nor extortioners, shall inherit the kingdom of God. And such were some of you: but ye are washed, but ye are sanctified . . . in the name of the Lord Jesus."

She looked at Sally pleadingly, but she only stared away past Peggy's gaze, her eyes defiant and two red splotches discoloring her cheeks.

Peggy looked at the words again as she started to close the book. But as she did she was struck by the awfulness of their meaning and the abyss they opened, an abyss on which Sally was so clearly teetering. She leaned across the table and said earnestly, "I do so much want you to let the Lord Jesus wash and cleanse you!" She didn't know if the words would have any meaning for Sally, but she couldn't keep them from bursting out.

Sally's only response was a cloud of cigarette smoke and a tight-lipped answer. "I tell you, I won't have you preaching at me!"

She stood up abruptly and looked down at Peggy. "Go on back to your world. You don't belong in mine. And don't bother calling me again. I've had it with your sermons."

Peggy watched miserably as Sally stalked out of the restaurant, pushing through the door to the street without a backward glance. It had seemed so right and necessary to say what she had that it was dismaying to see it had had the wrong result.

When she met Jane, one look at her face was enough. "It didn't go so well, huh?"

Peggy shook her head. "I thought I was doing it just right, but it turned out all wrong. I did get her phone number, but she'll probably hang up if I try to call her."

She called Ann that evening to report the failure and asked, "Do you think I should try to see her again?"

"I don't think it would help, Peggy. She sounded pretty final. After all, we can't make her do what she doesn't want to."

It was just after lunch on Friday that Miss Murphy called her to the phone.

It was Sally and she began abruptly, "How did you happen to find me the other day? I didn't tell you where I worked."

"Sherlock Holmes stuff. Jane was with me and we walked up one street and down another until we found the right place," Peggy answered.

"Why? Why did you bother?"

"Because I care about you."

She didn't know how Sally would react to that. And because she didn't want to do anything to antagonize her, she waited for her response, praying that she had said the right thing this time.

"Where do I meet you for this thing tonight?"

Sally's voice was so casual and the question so unexpected that it took Peggy a moment to even make sense out of the words. Then she squeaked, "You're coming?"

"You invited me."

The coolness of Sally's voice warned Peggy not to get sentimental about it. "So I did. Well, I'm getting a ride and we'll pick you up."

"Better be careful. This isn't the right neighborhood for a Cadillac."

"Don't worry. We'll be in a beat-up Chevy. Quarter of eight OK?"

"I'll be out in front."

"Don't do that. Anton will come up—"

But Sally cut her short. "If you're on time, I'll be on time," and Peggy heard the receiver slam down.

She tore up to Jane's room and barged in. "Guess what! That was Sally and she's coming!"

7

The Club Meeting

PEGGY WAS SO AFRAID they might be late and make Sally change her mind that she called Anton and asked if he would mind coming early. Then they got to Sally's neighborhood too soon and had to park along a side street for twenty minutes. Peggy's nerves were so edgy that she looked suspiciously at everyone who walked past the car. Finally it was time and they pulled up in front of the apartment building just as Sally stepped out the door.

She thought the ride to the Vanacek's was one of the longest she had ever taken. Anton never did talk very much, and tonight he was more silent than usual. Peggy, so nervous about the outcome of the evening for Ann and herself as well as for Sally, couldn't concentrate on keeping a conversation going. And Sally sat in one corner of the back seat smoking and seeming not to need to talk. Again, remembering the bubbling warmth and candor of another Sally, Peggy found herself silently begging for Mrs. Tremont's miracle to take place—somehow.

They pulled up in front of Anton's house and got out of the car with Sally looking around her suspiciously.

"Is this where the meeting is?" she demanded.

"I'm sorry. I forgot you don't know Lisa or what this is all about."

Sally started to say something in reply and then shook her head and walked silently up to the porch.

"Everyone's probably out in the kitchen," Anton said as he held the screen door open and motioned them in. "This is the night for a cooking lesson and my mother is showing them how to make something."

Peggy sniffed. "Um, smells wonderful."

Anton shrugged. "Just like always when my mother cooks."

Standing in the narrow, dark front hall, Peggy looked toward the kitchen, dreading to walk its short length and become involved in the uncertainties of the lives clustered around the stove and sink. She could feel the palms of her hands damp with nervousness.

Then Ann, hearing them, came to the kitchen doorway. Her "Hi, come on out. We've just gotten started. That delicious smell is onion and stuff browning," didn't help Peggy's nervousness because Ann sounded so breathless and unsure of herself. Her voice, so falsely friendly and bright, did nothing to settle the butterflies in Peggy's stomach.

As they moved over and could be seen in the light of the kitchen, Ann gestured toward Peggy and said, "Kids, this is Lisa's friend I was telling you about. And her friend," she added, nodding in Sally's direction.

Peggy looked around at the faces turned toward them and was sure it wasn't her imagination that the main expression on each was suspicious hostility. *Maybe this was a mistake after all*, she thought in panic when she saw that the eyes which had shifted to Sally were more hostile than ever. *Ann was right; Sally isn't going t* *fit in, and she might end up spoiling Ann's chance* *with these girls.*

But it was too late to back out now so she said "Hi," and then cleared her throat at the squeaky sound that came out.

Nobody responded to her timid greeting. Then Mrs Vanacek broke the uncomfortable moment with a quick and impatient, "Come, get busy if you expect to eat this tonight. Whichever one is peeling potatoes, finish. Are the onions ready yet? You there with the wooden spoon, use it, don't just stand and hold it."

Standing on the fringe of the project, Peggy caught her breath at the sharpness in Mrs. Vanacek's voice, expecting somebody to get mad and throw something. Any one of them looked as though she could pull a knife and use it at a moment's notice. She looked around nervously and then scolded herself for being so melodramatic. The girl with the enormous soft brown eyes who was peeling potatoes was certainly sweet-looking.

Leaving Sally slouching in the doorway, she went over to the sink and picked up a knife to help. After a few minutes the girl said, "Hey, where'd you learn to use a knife like that?"

It was only then that Peggy noticed how awkwardly the other girl had been peeling the potato, slicing deep pieces away with the skin and leaving only a small part of the potato.

"Years of practice," Peggy answered offhandedly. "I've got a brother who never reaches bottom when it comes to food. So bread and potatoes are the least expensive way to fill him up, and potatoes you have to peel."

She knew the minute she said the words that she'd made a mistake making even the least reference to money. The faded jeans and torn canvas shoes with the broken laces of the other girl were typical of what they all were wearing. But all she could do was to go on working while she felt the eyes looking her up and down, taking in the lime green slacks and sweater and the matching patent shoes.

She had had a hard time deciding what to wear until Jane had said, "Just wear what you would if you were going to something with your own friends. Wearing something old and ragged isn't going to fool them into thinking you come from as hard a background as they do. It might make them mad if they thought you're a phony."

Now she knew how right Jane had been because it would have taken more than just old clothes for her to look like these girls. She could have put on faded jeans and canvas shoes. But she couldn't pretend the hardness and sophistication they assumed, no matter how she tried, because she wouldn't want to. Conscious of the tension charging the air around her, she went on calmly peeling potatoes, though her hands shook slightly, hoping she hadn't caused the whole evening to fall apart.

Then one of the girls said, "Relax! I've got three brothers like that. But it's a good thing Goofy here doesn't, because she couldn't learn to peel anything no matter how much practice she had."

"Says who?" And Peggy saw that the huge brown

eyes were not soft now but glinted with dangerous sparks.

"Says me! And don't try to make something out of it!"

The two girls faced each other, each with a knife held ready, and Peggy wondered what could ever save this from being a disaster.

It was Mrs. Vanacek who sharply interrupted again. "You remember the bargain you made with Lisa. If you want to fight, go home. You don't break up my house and get blood all over my clean kitchen. Hear?"

Peggy swallowed hard at the words. This could have been for real after all. She wondered how Mrs. Vanacek dared speak so crossly. What if they turned on her? But she obviously knew what she was doing because she had turned immediately back to sifting flour, expecting to be obeyed. And she was, after the girls had glared at each other a moment longer.

Then, remembering Sally, Peggy looked around and found her watching Ann who was frowning over a recipe for making noodles.

"If it's that hard for you, why not just buy some?" Sally demanded.

Ann laughed. "That's the way I would do it. But the boss here doesn't think 'boughten' noodles do justice to her glop. They have to be the real thing. But I've never made any before and I'm too chicken to start."

"Just follow the recipe," Mrs. Vanacek ordered her as sharply as she had spoken a few minutes before to the troublemakers, and Ann as meekly obeyed.

Peggy watched as Ann measured and sifted and stirred and sliced and was surprised to hear Sally, still leaning back against the wall as she had been ever

ince they got there, order, "Sift it again," and "Hey,
ut those strips thinner."

"How come you know so much about making
noodles?" Peggy asked curiously.

Sally shrugged. "I've made millions of them with my
grandmother."

"Well, for Pete's sake! You do them then," Ann exclaimed as she thrust the bowl of dough at Sally.

Sally shook her head with a curt "No thanks. I'm just
a visitor. I'm strictly from outside."

"Yeah? What'd you come for then?" demanded the
girl with the brown eyes whom someone had called
Tanya.

Watching Sally closely, Peggy could almost hear the
words forming in her mind and shaping on her lips,
For laughs, and she found herself begging silently,
Please, Sally, don't say that!

Sally hadn't been looking at her, but now as she
glanced in her direction, Peggy looked at her warningly.
After a moment Sally shrugged again and said, "Because Lisa's friend made me."

This was apparently the least offensive thing she
could have said, even though her voice was sarcastic,
because Tanya went back to what she was doing and
no one else asked any questions. The rest of the meal
was fixed with a minimum of argument.

Peggy never did find out what the dish was really
called but it was delicious with the thick slices of
homemade bread that Mrs. Vanacek piled in a large
basket in the middle of the table. She lost count of
how many times the basket was emptied and refilled
and wondered uneasily how Mrs. Vanacek could afford

to feed the ravenous appetites of the eight girls aroun
the table very often.

Sally was the only sour note during the meal, re
fusing the plate that Mrs. Vanacek ladled full for he
"I'm not hungry," she said flatly in answer to Mr
Vanacek's blunt "You are too skinny." And nothin
would budge her. Peggy was sure she must be hungr
from the way she watched the rest of them eat, but a
she would take was a cup of black coffee and her eve
present cigarette.

Watching her, Peggy thought, *She's a lot mor
stubborn than I expected. She's not going to see he
need of Christ very easily.* And a thread of discourage
ment crept through her. Mrs. Tremont had warned
about this, of course. The old Sally, Peggy remem
bered suddenly, had been stubborn too, listening to
what she had timidly said about being a Christian
but carelessly shrugging it off for herself. There was
no reason to think that time or circumstances had
made this Sally any more pliable. The only comfort
in it was that if she ever did give in and accept the
Lord, she might be as stubborn for Him as she was
now against Him.

Because she still felt uneasy and at a loss to know
how to talk to the girls, and because Sally pointedly
ignored her, Peggy stayed on the edge of the group
during the meal, watching and listening. But nobody
talked much, for the girls all concentrated on eating,
each one making sure she got as much as the person
beside her.

When they finally finished eating and shoved their
plates away, Peggy was glad it was Ann and not she
who had the responsibility for the rest of the evening.

She knew she wouldn't have any idea what to say to them, and she hoped Ann did.

She watched as Ann, without moving from the table, shoved her chair back, leaned down and pulled a guitar out from under the buffet behind her and smiled around at the circle of faces.

"OK, who wants to sing what?" she asked.

Peggy hadn't realized how tense she was until she felt her muscles relaxing at the sound of Ann's voice. The uncertainty and fear had been replaced by assurance, and her smile was warm and friendly.

"You gonna be like Lisa and not let us sing any of the songs we know?" The girl who asked the question didn't sound resentful, only curious.

Ann smiled back at her as she strummed a few notes on the guitar and said, "Since this is really Lisa's party, I don't want to do anything she wouldn't do. I'm expecting all of you to steer me in the right direction. Probably Lisa and I know the same songs, but maybe you and I don't. If I learn yours, will you learn mine?"

"Sure," the girl said and reached for the guitar. She strummed a few measures and then began a love song with particularly suggestive words, singing it in a low, sultry, and not very good voice.

She was stopped by a crash in the ribs from the girl beside her who said in disgust, "For crying out loud! That's the only kind you know. Give that back." And she grabbed the guitar and handed it to Ann.

They sang a couple of rock numbers the girls asked for, with Ann picking out enough notes to give unity to the voices, and then several choruses Lisa had taught them. Then Tanya took the guitar. She began to strum softly with her eyes closed and then gradually her body swayed in time to the gentle rhythm. There were no words at first, only a melancholy, haunting melody that swelled and ebbed in a cadence almost unbearably sweet. Then Tanya put words to the music and sang one of the saddest, sweetest love songs Peggy had ever heard. The words asked questions about life, looked for answers, but ended in despair. At the first line Ann drew in her breath sharply and leaned forward, listening intently until the music stopped on a mournful, minor note.

"Hey, that's a new one," one of the girls finally said into the stillness that gripped them. "Where'd you learn it?"

Tanya shrugged. "My aunt's just up from the hills and she sings it all the time. She's about to drive us all nuts with it." There was mockery in her voice but along with it a wistful longing that made tears sting Peggy's eyes.

But Ann had reached for the guitar and said, "I like the second verse even better than the first," and sang it through in the same gentle, swaying rhythm and with the same mournful, haunting notes Tanya had used, except that her voice gave it a beauty it hadn't had when Tanya sang it.

"Where'd *you* learn it?" The question was asked half in surprise and half in anger.

Ann caught the shade of anger in Tanya's voice and said contritely, "I'm sorry, I didn't mean to steal your song, but I've been crazy to hear it sung. My boyfriend has been down in the hills all summer and he sent me the words in one of his letters and said he wished he could send me the music because it was absolutely out of this world, and that he'd sing it for me when he got home. So when you started singing those words, I couldn't believe it. I only know those two verses. Are there more?"

Tanya nodded and Ann held out the guitar. "Sing them, will you?"

But Tanya shook her head and looked away stiffly.

"Please?" Ann begged.

"I don't know the others very good."

"Sing the first two verses then again," Ann begged. "There's such a terrific idea behind the words. This thing of 'needing help from someone, somewhere' is what bothers everyone, no matter who they are. Some people look for it in love, and some people in money, and some people even think they'll find it in dope. I know Lisa has told you that she found Jesus Christ is the only One who can really help. I've found that too. It's just tremendous to know that God loves you and that He'll help you in everything if you will just let Him."

Peggy was watching the girls' faces as they listened and thought she had never seen such absolute blank reaction. They just listened—that was all.

Ann still held the guitar out to Tanya who shook her head and said, "I don't sing good enough."

"Oh. Well, let's everybody sing then." Ann was a good leader and played well, but the enthusiasm the girls had had earlier was gone. Ann started another song but stopped when no one joined in.

"What's the matter? Lisa said this was one you really liked. What am I doing wrong? Is it pitched too high?"

"You sing too good for us," one of the girls answered. "We don't sing so hot, but neither does Lisa, so we can goof around with her."

"Well, look, I won't sing then," Ann began.

"It's not you," Tanya interrupted. "It's just that we don't want to sing with you listening."

The evening was over suddenly then in a rush when one of the girls stood up quickly. "Gotta go. Got a ride waiting for me."

"Her and her rides," someone else said scornfully. "She's going to wake up dead someday from one of her rides."

"So it's her business." The voice, bitter and biting, was Sally's, and the other girl whirled to glare at her.

"Sure it's her business," she snapped. "So what's it to you? She's *my* friend and I can make her business my business if I want to." She stopped in front of Sally, her hands on her hips, and stared theateningly at her.

Peggy gulped in dismay, but Sally only stared coldly back, slouched carelessly in her chair by the dining room window, and blew cigarette smoke up in the girl's face. A couple of the others grabbed their friend's arm and pulled her out of the house, slamming the screen door behind them. Outside, their voices were loud in denouncing the girl who was still waiting for her ride. It seemed strangely empty in the house as Ann put the guitar away and Peggy looked thoughtfully at Sally. How odd that she had been such a misfit and so resented by these girls to whom life was such a grim struggle.

She turned from her absentminded musing about Sally as Ann said, "I sure blew that! The whole evening fizzled."

"Nah, they got what they came for—the food," Sally said cynically. She got up and strolled to the kitchen door where she stood leaning against it looking at the stack of unwashed dishes and cooking pans.

"Why didn't you make them clean up their mess before they left?" She threw the question back over her shoulder at Ann.

"I-I-I don't know," she answered uncertainly. "Lisa didn't say she made them wash dishes. I was afraid to be too strict for fear they would get mad and not want to come back. I didn't want to spoil all Lisa had done—" Her voice trailed off under Sally's withering stare.

"Nuts!" Sally retorted contemptuously. "Whenever I had a bunch over, my mother made sure I let everyone know they were expected to clean up after them." She stopped, aware of what she was saying and glanced at Peggy. Then she tossed her hair back over her shoulder and went on defiantly.

"That's just the way all you do-gooders are. You're just too sweet and goody-goody. If you let these punk kids take advantage of you, you'll never get anywhere with them. You've got to be as tough as they are. Take that one who tried to outstare me. If she had thought I was scared of her, she'd have socked me. You won't accomplish anything by giving in to them."

"Just what do you think we are trying to accomplish with them?" Ann asked the question quietly, and Peggy listened intently for the answer. It might give a clue to what else she might be able to say to Sally.

But Sally only gave her familiar, careless shrug as she rolled up her sleeves and turned on the hot water faucet. "It doesn't really matter much, because you're not going to make it with them no matter what you're aiming for." Her voice was loud over the running water. "The problem is that you're just not on the same level with them. You don't talk the same language. You have to really learn to think and feel the way they do, not just the way *you* think they think or the way *you* think they feel. And you'll never get to them by these little slumming parties you're having, either," she finished scornfully.

"I don't think you've got it quite straight," Ann began, but Sally turned off the water and faced her, her voice thick with disgust.

"Look, I don't know who this Lisa is or was or how come you happened to pick this place to have these meetings, but I can tell you it will never work. Oh, sure, this place *looks* slummy enough. But all you do is come here from your nice little safe rich world and then go right back to it and forget about this dump until next week when it's time for another little soup-kettle-and-preaching service for the have-nots. I know all about how you think. I know because I lived in the so-called safe, rich world once. But I'm glad I had the nerve to get out of it."

There was a loud commotion at the front door as Sally finished and they heard the screen door slam shut. Then feet pounded down from upstairs and Anton whispered urgently, "Pa! Pa! Come here!"

But the feet shuffled along the hall to the kitchen door and the girls stared at the swaying figure of the unshaven, bleary-eyed, dirty drunk who blinked in the bright light. He shrugged off Anton's hand on his arm with a thick, slurred, "Lemme 'lone. Can stand

all 'lone. Gonna talk to girls," and he lurched forward
and grabbed Ann's arm, pulling her toward him with
a leering, "C'mere, honey. Wanna talk."

Mrs. Vanacek said sharply, "Stop!"

Her husband turned toward her and, letting go of
Ann, lunged toward her with his fist raised. Anton
reached out quickly and grabbed his father's arm,
holding him as he lost his balance and his knees
buckled. Mrs. Vanacek took the other arm and, between them, they turned the sagging figure around
and led him back down the hall. The girls stood frozen,
listening to the laborious, stumbling progress up the
stairs with Mr. Vanacek pouring out curses at his wife
and son. And all the time Peggy was seeing Lisa's
lovely face and wondering how many times she had
seen this kind of thing as she grew up, and Mrs.
Vanacek's determination to keep her children un-
spotted from their father's life, and Anton's driving
ambition to have a different life. Finally the doors
slammed shut upstairs and it was quiet.

"Well, who was *that* character?"

Peggy turned on Sally. Her eyes glinted sparks and
her voice shook with anger. "That's the best answer
I could give you for your fancy speech. This is the
house Lisa has lived in all her life, and that was her
father and this is a sample of the kind of life they
have always had with him. He never is sober. Lots
of times they've been hungry because he spent all his
money on drink. They wouldn't even have had clothes
to wear if their mother hadn't gone out and done
laundry and cleaned houses for other people. Lisa has
always lived in this slum and she knows what she's

doing when she tries to help these girls get out of this kind of life.

"You think you know so much!" she continued scornfully. "You're the one who doesn't know how people feel when they've hit bottom. You chose the kind of life you're in and you can get out of it any time you want to. You're the one doing the slumming, not us. These girls you are so superior to were born in this kind of life and they can't leave it any time they get tired of it. You can. Lisa made it out because she became a Christian and had help from God and that's the only way these girls will make it out."

And then, hardly knowing that Ann and Sally were staring at her as though hypnotized, Peggy leaned forward across the kitchen table, gripping the edge until her knuckles were white. "You asked where we expected to get with them. I'll tell you. We're trying to get them to see that they need the Lord Jesus as their Saviour. He's the only One who can give them hope and a new life. And let me tell you that that's the only way you'll ever get out of your dirty little pretend world!"

She stopped then, shaking with tears and anger and there was silence. Then Anton said from the doorway, "I'll take you girls home whenever you're ready."

8

Sally Listens

THE RIDE HOME was strained and silent. Peggy was afraid to say anything more for fear she would find herself apologizing for what she had already said. And she would not do that because it had all been true. Sally sat staring out the window, her face absolutely expressionless, saying nothing. When Anton stopped the car in front of Sally's building, she managed a weak, " 'Bye, Sally. Thanks for coming."

But Sally didn't answer, didn't even glance in her direction. She simply reached for the door handle and then stopped to look up and down the street before getting out. The streetlight in front of her building was broken but lights shone from the first floor apartment where four men, the window shades up, were playing cards and drinking. Two couples were sitting on the steps of the apartment building next door. Down at the corner another couple was in the midst of a screaming argument, the young wife balancing a crying baby on her hip while her husband shoved her along the sidewalk.

Anton shut off the motor, took the keys out of the ignition and said to Sally, "I'm walking up with you."

"Don't bother!" she snapped.

Anton ignored her and said to Peggy, "Lock the doors when we get out. I'll just walk her up to her door and be right back."

"I tell you, you don't have to," Sally said again as he came around and held the door for her.

"Come on," he ordered.

Anton's caution made Peggy even more nervous. If he was that concerned when he was used to this kind of atmosphere, the neighborhood must be dangerous; that made Sally's living here all the worse.

She leaned forward to watch as they crossed the sidewalk and entered the building, and then waited for a light to shine from Sally's window. She shuddered as she remembered the dark stairway and then began to worry about Anton. What if there was someone like his father lurking in the dark? Suddenly she saw a light go on, saw Sally's figure at the window as she pulled down the shade, and then sighed with relief as Anton hurried out of the building and to the car.

He unlocked it and got in quickly, shaking his head as he started the motor and pulled away from the curb. "I sure don't see why she wants to live in a crummy place like this when she's got such a nice home."

Peggy looked at him, wondering how he knew where Sally lived. He felt her glance and said, "I work on a package service that delivers for a lot of different department stores. We had a delivery at her place just today. They buy a lot of stuff, so we make trips there pretty often. I'm the one who usually goes to the door with the packages. She's got a couple of cute sisters."

His voice was noncommital as he went on, "One

of them especially always talks a lot when she signs for packages. A couple of weeks ago she asked how come I wasn't on the truck the day before. I told her I didn't work that day because my sister got married. She said something about 'My sister Sally' and then sort of clammed up all of a sudden. So I put two and two together and came up with this Sally when I found out the last name was the same."

"Anton, is this place where she's living really dangerous? I mean, could she get hurt just living here?"

He shrugged his shoulders. "Anyplace can be dangerous, I suppose. You read in the papers about things that happen even in ritzy neighborhoods like the one where your aunt lives. But it's worse in places like this—and the one where I live. Places like your aunt's have their own swimming pools and tennis courts; and if you don't like it there, you can always go someplace else—to a club or something. Where we are, the kids stand around without anything to do. There aren't any parks and pools close by and they don't have money to go anyplace. So one guy gets an idea of how to work up some excitement just for something to do, and then the next guy has to go him one better, and they end up breaking the law. Then they get hauled in and get a police record that stays with them forever." He drove in a brooding silence for a few blocks.

Then he said, "Or maybe they get hopped up on drugs, again just for kicks maybe, and get in trouble because they don't know what they're doing. It doesn't even have to be drugs or glue-sniffing or things like that. Just liquor will do it. Too much of that stuff can fix anybody. And it ruins life for everyone in the family." His voice was bitter and sad at the same time, and Peggy felt like crying at the thought of what Lisa and he had lived through.

But her thoughts came back to worry about Sally. "What will happen to her if she stays where she is?"

He shrugged again, but his voice was tight. "Nothing good, believe me. If she's not on drugs now, she will be if she stays there long. She'd better get out of it while she can."

"But she won't listen to anybody," Peggy protested tearfully.

"Then she'll have to learn the hard way—by experience. Maybe that sounds heartless, but it's the only way some people learn."

They drove the rest of the way in silence with Peggy too drained emotionally to talk anymore.

The sick feeling she took to bed with her was there when she woke up the next morning. She had hoped that things wouldn't look so bad after a night's sleep, but the memory of the way she had blazed out still made her cringe. If only she had kept still and just let Sally talk, or had waited for Ann to answer, because she was always cool and sensible. But no, she had to be the one to lose her good judgment and bawl Sally out. It didn't matter that she had needed it if it meant she would never again let anyone talk to her about Christ.

Peggy turned over and buried her face in the pillow to shut out the morning light, but she knew she couldn't go back to sleep even though it was early. This business of thinking you were the only one with answers for everyone only caused trouble. And yet— she did have the answer for Sally, if only she could

be made to see it. Regardless of what that early
experience had been, whether it had been a real
conversion or not, she was certainly in a desperate
condition now.

She got up and wandered over to the window,
pushing aside the frilly curtains to look out across the
sunbathed lawn to the curve of the garden where the
roses were banked against the low hedges in a scarlet
mass of color. But in her mind the green and crimson
and gold of the lawn and flowers were wiped out by
the memory of the dirt-littered streets and faded
houses she had seen last night. She heard again the
pitiful wailing of the baby caught in the noise and
anger of its quarreling parents.

She tried to remember what the girls looked like
as they sat around the table eating, but their faces
blanked together fuzzily in her memory. They were
not individual people to her, but a group, all alike.
Only Sally stood out for her—separate, needy, lost. It
wasn't fair that she should be more concerned about
Sally than about the others. But she could not forget
the bond she had felt for her that day so long ago
when—shy, timid, afraid—she had hesitatingly explained why she was a Christian and had still been
accepted for herself with no questions or ridicule. God
must have had a purpose in bringing them together
again after so many years and with such a slim tie
binding them. That was why she had such an aching
sense of failure for having been impatient with Sally
only out of loyalty for Lisa. She had to admit honestly
that it was Sally's attack on Lisa that had prompted
her anger. And Lisa would be the last person in the

world to want her loyalty if it meant losing out on a witness to someone in need of Christ.

The details of last night's scenes repeated themselves in her mind again, and she saw the swaying figure and heard Mr. Vanacek's thick speech and the stumbling of his feet up the stairs. She felt again her anger that this should be Lisa's father. She heard the pain and anger in Anton's voice as he talked about his life. And yet, out of this life Lisa and Anton had come to Christ.

Still staring unseeingly at the beautiful view, Peggy went back through the years. Of all her friends who had become Christians, Alice and Phyllis stood out, each so different from the other. Phyllis had lost everything that seemed important to her, and it was easy to understand the hopelessness that had brought her to the edge of death from a deliberate overdose of sleeping pills. But Alice too had come to the same place of despair although she hadn't shown it in as dramatic a way as Phyllis had. Her desperation had been quieter, though no less intense.

Yet it didn't matter which of them had been the more desperate and in need of help, because in the end both of them had been reached by the same invitation—"Come unto me . . . and ye shall find rest unto your souls." This was a strange invitation to offer the restless, turbulent girls who had been at Lisa's last night. And yet, it was what they needed most. And so did Sally.

Peggy turned to look at the calendar on the desk. The trouble was there was so little time. A week from Monday they would be leaving for home. And

Sally had gotten out of the car last night without looking at her or answering her timid good night.

As she showered and dressed, she finally brought out and examined the other problem that was the main reason for her discouragement. It was her mother. She was the most unreachable of all. The discouragement Peggy felt about Sally she knew was bound up really in her mother's adamant stand against anything connected with Christianity.

Mrs. Andrews had gone to church the first Sunday of the visit and then had steadfastly turned aside any further invitations, outwardly polite. But Peggy was sure that inside she seethed with resentment whenever another invitation was given. She had gone to several luncheons with Aunt Emily and her friends and had come home unmoved by what she had heard—except for anger that she had been forced to listen. Peggy didn't know what her mother and aunt talked about the times they sat together in the lazy afternoons, her mother absorbed in the sweater she was making for Bill's birthday next month. They talked, Peggy knew, because she had seen them. But she was sure any attempt her aunt made to talk about Christ would end in failure. Her mother would simply close off any discussion with that fixed white line around her mouth and her nostrils pinched with suppressed anger. Even Aunt Emily would not be able to penetrate the barrier.

She remembered the end of one conversation between them she had overheard when her aunt had said in that assured way her mother would find aggravating almost beyond endurance, "Well, Elizabeth, you'll just have to see the light the way I did. I once

was as blind to it as you are. When Walter became
a Christian, I was terribly angry. The only thing that
kept me from divorcing him was the thought of how
our friends would talk. Fortunately he helped me see
my need of Christ too. We have a stubborn heritage,
Elizabeth, and we won't admit what we don't want
to—that we need help beyond our own ability." Then
she had added with a sad smile, "The trouble is that
in holding to our stubbornness too long we sometimes
lose things that are very precious."

The memory of these words weighed on Peggy now
with an insistent sense of time being lost for both her
mother and Sally. On impulse, she dialed Sally's
number, hoping she didn't work on Saturday.

There was no answer and as she put the phone
down, Jane stuck her head in the door. "Hi! How'd
it go last night? Sorry I went to bed before you got
home."

"It was awful! I'm sorry I even took her," Peggy
answered and poured out the story.

"Maybe when she has a chance to think over what
you said, she won't be mad. I'd keep trying to reach
her if I were you," Jane advised.

Peggy did try at different times during the week
with no success until finally about the middle of
Saturday morning a sleepy voice answered, "Hello?"

"Sally! I'm so glad you're home. I've been trying
to get you all week."

There was silence at the other end of the line and
Peggy held her breath, afraid she would hang up.

Finally Sally asked rudely, "What for?"

"I wanted to see you again before we leave."

"When are you going?"

"Monday."

"Oh."

The word was said so impersonally that it carried neither interest nor regret. Peggy didn't know exactly what she had expected, but certainly some kind of interest would have been at least polite. But apparently a veneer of politeness was something that Sally had thrown off along with all the other external features of her former life. Peggy bit her lip, wondering if she should carry through with the invitation she had intended to give when she had dialed Sally's number so hopefully. She could hear Sally breathing and a faint sound which indicated she was blowing cigarette smoke. Finally she blurted, "I wish you'd do me a favor—"

She stopped and Sally said, "Maybe. What is it?"

"Come to church with us tomorrow."

"Don't you really mean that you'll be doing *me* a favor?" Sally's voice was so mocking that Peggy winced.

But she made herself answer calmly, "I hope it will turn out to be a favor for you too. That's the main reason I'm asking, of course. But we want you to come to dinner after church too. This may be the last time we'll see each other, because I don't expect to come here again, and who knows if you will ever visit me?"

This time there was such a long silence at the other end of the line that Peggy finally said, "Sally? Are you there?"

"What church is it? The one Mrs. Tremont goes to?"

"No, my aunt's."

"You *want* me to come?"

Peggy let out her breath in a soundless sigh of relief. Instead of the flat refusal or the mocking answer she had expected, there was a faintly pleading note in Sally's voice.

"Yes! I would have asked you a couple of weeks ago if I had thought you might come. Will you?"

"Do I have to fix my hair?"

"Yes, wash it and comb it," Peggy retorted, surprised at the question and hoping Sally would take the answer in its light vein—but seriously.

"How and where do I meet you?"

"We'll pick you up. Ten-thirty sharp OK?"

"I'll watch out the window and come down as soon as I see you. Which Cadillac will it be this time?"

Peggy smiled at the derisive note in Sally's voice. Mocking the rich—including her own family—was one of the habits she had assumed in this new identity she was trying. So Peggy answered casually, "The third oldest probably. See you at ten-thirty." She hung up, hardly believing the conversation was real.

Since Jane wasn't there and she simply had to share the news with someone, she stopped at her aunt's room, knocked, and went in when her aunt answered.

"I just talked to Sally and she's coming! I can't believe that she really agreed. Thanks *so* much for letting me invite her."

"You know you are welcome, my dear."

"The thing is," Peggy said hesitantly, "she will probably want to smoke all afternoon. She does almost all the time, though I don't think she realizes it."

Her aunt's smile was sad as she answered, "You know this house has had its share of cigarette smoke

and the smell of liquor. It won't matter if it happens
again. Don't let it worry you. What did you say Sally's
last name is?"

"Sanders."

"Is her father a lawyer?"

"I don't know. I've never heard her say."

"Your uncle has gotten to know a Mr. Sanders
quite well this past year. He has been handling some
of the company's legal work and doing it very well.
We don't know them socially, though he and your
uncle have golfed together at the club. Walter had
heard he was having family troubles, but I'm sure he
had no idea of the extent—if he is Sally's father. It's
sad to think of some of the burdens people carry
with no one to help them. The saddest part, of course,
is that God would help if they would let Him."

"I feel so burdened for Sally and yet so helpless
too because I don't know how to talk to her about
the Lord. She cuts me off every time I try. I guess
that's why I'm so surprised that she's willing to come
to church."

"Doesn't the Bible say that God will reward the
prayer of the person who prays faithfully even if he
doesn't seem to get any results?" Aunt Emily's voice
was groping and uncertain, and Peggy smiled back at
her gratefully.

"Sometimes I forget that though." Then Peggy
looked at her aunt soberly. "I guess you know what
I pray about most—and longest and hardest."

Her aunt nodded. "Just remember you are not alone
in it, my dear. I am praying it with you. You see,
Peggy, I have so much to make up to your mother—
more than you can ever possibly imagine. I know that

praying for her salvation now will not erase my years
of neglect of her. Yes, and my cruelty too. I must
confess that often there was that, though it was sometimes unintentional."

Peggy felt the tears in her own eyes as she watched
her aunt's trembling lips and saw the pain that clouded
her eyes. Then she went on, "But there doesn't seem
to be any way I can reach through to her until she
is saved. I've tried so many ways during these weeks.
This, of course, is one of the reasons I wanted you to
visit. She is so remote—so closed off—that I can't
reach through to her either by words or actions. She
is pleasant when I talk, but so distant that I know
my words mean nothing to her. She clings so to past
wrongs that she refuses to let them be righted."

Peggy nodded. She had thought this too—that her
mother was afraid to let go of her bitterness.

But then her aunt said more briskly, "But when
she does yield to Christ, she will see things in a
different light. Her salvation won't erase the mistakes
and misunderstandings of the past, but it will help to
make them endurable."

Peggy caught hopefully at the last few sentences
as she said eagerly, "You said *when* she yields. Do
you really think she will?"

Her aunt got up to move restlessly around the room,
her hands caught together tightly and her voice agitated as she said, "She must! She must!" Then she
turned to face Peggy and said more quietly, "God has
given us assurance in His Word that He will answer
prayer if we ask in faith and do not doubt."

Peggy nodded in answer, but she left the room un-
comforted. No matter how hard they prayed they

could not make her mother do what she didn't want to do; God would not force her to accept Christ against her will.

Her discouragement was deepened by her mother's refusal again to go to church with them the next day. To Peggy she said privately and angrily, "Let's not spoil the last hours we are here arguing about this matter. *I am not going.* I fulfilled my duty by going the first Sunday we were here, and that's enough."

To her sister's invitation, she said merely, "I'll stay home and get partially packed. I dislike doing things in a rush at the last minute, and I'm afraid that's what we will be doing on Monday."

Peggy was sure her mother had been practically packed for several days in her eagerness to be out from under her sister's roof. But she didn't want her aunt to know that, so she said, "You can start on my things if you want to."

"I think I'd better. If you have your friend here all afternoon, you won't have time to do a decent job. There's an art to packing a suitcase so that everything doesn't get wrinkled."

"I guess my philosophy is that there's always an iron at the other end of the trip," Peggy laughed.

She was nervous about the whole thing as she brushed her teeth after breakfast on Sunday and dressed. Perhaps it was just as well her mother wasn't going. It was going to be hard enough to concentrate on Sally and her reactions to the service without having to worry about her mother too.

As Peggy gave her uncle directions to Sally's place, he turned a startled look at her. "She lives there? Does her family know it?"

"No. And—please don't tell her father," she begged. "I promised I wouldn't."

He said no more but shook his head in unbelief as he stopped in front of Sally's building and looked around. She came from the shelter of the doorway and got into the back seat beside Peggy. Peggy hadn't dared think how Sally might look and was relieved that she didn't appear to be quite as much of a cast-off waif as she had looked every other time they had been together. She had her hair done in a French twist and wore a pale yellow linen suit that was well made, though it hung loosely on her thin body. It must have come with her from home. Peggy wondered if she had more of her own clothes with her and only wore the dirty rags as a part of the picture she was trying to create.

She nodded at Jane and spoke briefly as she was introduced to the others. "I met you once a long time ago," she said to Aunt Emily. "When Peggy visited here before."

Uncle Walter said, "I know your father. He does business with me. He's a fine man."

Peggy saw the closed look that came over Sally's face and wondered if that had been a wise thing for him to say. But Sally only turned to Peggy and asked abruptly, "Where's your mother?"

"She decided to stay home and get ready to leave tomorrow. Our train goes at ten in the morning and Mother's the kind who has to be at the station an hour or two ahead of time. I'm the kind who runs up just in time to clamber onto the caboose—if I'm lucky enough to even make that."

"Which passenger trains don't have, silly," Jane scoffed.

"Well, whatever is last I'm apt to be on it."

They pulled into a parking space in the lot behind the church and got out of the car. Peggy didn't suppose the outside of the church building would impress Sally the way it had her mother, who had looked appreciatively at the ivy-covered brick and stone building with its steeple and melodious chimes. But she fervently hoped the warm evangelistic service which had left her mother cold would do something for Sally.

She had expected her to either act bored to death or else look around superciliously and not hear anything that went on. Instead, she shared the hymnbook Peggy held over to her, bowed her head during the prayers and, outwardly at least, listened to the sermon. Her expression was so inscrutable Peggy couldn't imagine what she was thinking. She determined that somehow, someway, the afternoon must not slip away without Sally having been confronted again with the power of the Lord Jesus to transform her life.

9

A Telegram Arrives

THEY CAME OUT OF THE CHURCH into the warm sunshine and talked to a few of Jane's friends. Then Aunt
Emily came over to them, suggesting, "Perhaps we
shouldn't leave your mother alone too long on this
last day," and led the way to the car.

As Uncle Walter turned into the long winding driveway, Jane said impulsively, "Let's sit outside for a
while. Dinner won't be ready yet, will it?"

Aunt Emily looked at her watch. "I told Frances
one o'clock, and it's not yet twelve-thirty. Just be
careful to watch the time."

The girls strolled across the grass and sat down in
the lawn chairs beside the pool.

"I'm going to miss all this sunshine during the
cold gloomy winter months," Peggy said with a sigh.
"I'll be envying you two soaking it up and being so
used to it that you won't even appreciate it. I must
admit that your winter weather is better than ours."

"Why stay there? Why not come out here for college?" Sally rummaged in her purse for a cigarette,
hesitated, and then put it back, glancing furtively at
Peggy.

118

But Peggy paid no attention as she shook her head at Jane's quick "Hey, neat, Peggy. You could live here. That would be great!"

"In some ways it would be nice, but I don't want to go so far away from my family yet—" She stopped, contrite. She glanced at Sally and then away again, surprised to see that Sally's teeth were clamped on her lower lip as though to keep it from trembling.

To bridge the moment she went on. "Besides, I'm all accepted and I even know who my roommate will be. Her name is Sarah Elizabeth Montgomery. Isn't that pretty? And she says everyone calls her Liz which I think is terrible when she could be Betty, or Betsy, or Beth—"

"Or Sally. My name is really Sarah."

"I never think of you except as Sally and maybe you never thought that my name is Margaret. I'm hardly ever called that. My mother hates nicknames but even she is finally resigned to my being Peggy."

"So she took it out on poor me and gave me a name you couldn't shorten. I've always wanted a nickname but what can you do to glamorize plain old Jane?"

"Nicknames aren't so great. And anyway, I think people's names usually fit them." Sally got up as she spoke and dropped carelessly down on the grass on her back and put her arms under her head.

"Well, thanks!" Jane said.

But Peggy looked at Sally and thought, *Princess?* After a moment she said, "I suppose you know what your name means?"

"Oh, sure. I always thought it was a stupid meaning."

"That's OK. You're not one anyway," Peggy replied calmly, and Sally sat up abruptly, a flush on her thin cheeks.

"Look! One thing you never used to be was insulting," she exclaimed, and there was a quaver in her voice that Peggy was quick to notice.

"What are you two talking about?" Jane demanded. But neither of them answered as they stared at each other.

"I didn't mean to be insulting, and I'm sorry if it sounded like that. I just wanted somehow to shock you enough to make you listen to what I want to say, and this seemed like the best time and place to do it. You see, I *have* to tell you once more that you have to become a Christian or you will never get your life straightened out."

She held up a warning hand as Sally began to splutter, "Now look—"

"Please let me finish this while I've got nerve enough to do it. I'm sorry I got mad the other night, but I said things I really meant—things I really believe. I know you could get out of this life you're in and settle down and be OK and raise a decent family. But, Sally, that just isn't enough. If you only had some idea of the power God can give you to live better than you ever thought was possible, you wouldn't turn away from Him. You won't get this power any other way than by becoming His child through faith in Jesus Christ. He takes you just as you are and makes you into something special. Then you'll be able to live up to your name and really be a princess in God's sight."

Sally pulled grass aimlessly for a few minutes, her

head lowered so they couldn't see her face. Then, without looking up, she said to Jane, "You believe this too?"

Jane nodded. "Only I'm not as good at explaining it as Peggy is. I only know what Jesus did for me; and if He can make me different when I was such a selfish brat, He can change anyone, no matter who he is."

Again Sally was silent, and Peggy felt she had said all she could. She didn't want to pressure Sally into agreeing to something she didn't really believe just to get them off her back. So they sat in silence with Peggy praying desperately, *Please, God, help Sally to see that she needs You.*

Then Sally began slowly, "I never told you, but— a long time ago— the year after you were here before, I talked to Mrs. Tremont a few times and she told me some of this same stuff. And I—well, I said—well, you see, I thought she was pretty terrific and I wanted her to like me. So—so I said I believed what she was talking about. Only—I didn't really. I did go to church a few times—the one where she goes. But then, oh, I don't know what happened. I didn't get to know anyone there because we only went a couple of times and none of my friends went to church. So I quit. And then—" She gestured helplessly. "Nothing went right for me."

"It can though, Sally. You only have to believe that God loves you and that Jesus died for you."

"But how can I be sure that I wouldn't just be pretending?"

"Sally, God means it when He says that if we confess

our sins He will forgive them and cleanse us from
them. All that is necessary is for *you* to believe this.'

Peggy glanced at her watch, relieved to see that
it wasn't one o'clock yet and hoping nothing would
interrupt until Sally had had a chance to think this
through. And then Jane, facing the house, said, "It
must be time to go in. Miss Murphy is waving at us.'

Peggy looked around and felt bitter disappointment.
Just a few more minutes might have clinched it with
Sally. As they walked across the lawn toward the
house, she felt that once again an opportunity had
slipped away. Then she heard Jane say, "Miss Murphy
looks funny. Something must be wrong."

They had reached the edge of the driveway nearest
the front steps and Peggy looked at Miss Murphy who
stood at the top of the steps looking down at her. She
did look odd—so white. Peggy walked quickly up to
her and felt Miss Murphy's arm around her. She
looked beyond her through the open door into the
wide, cool hall where her mother stood motionless. A
piece of paper was clenched in her hand, and Peggy
felt her throat tighten with fear. She walked into the
house, hardly conscious of doing so.

"What is it?" she whispered. And then louder,
"Mother, what is it?"

Mrs. Andrews was like a stone, unhearing and
speechless, and Peggy took the paper from her un-
resisting hand and read the words. "Accident on road.
Bill seriously injured. Will phone home tonight."

It was Miss Murphy's handwriting, and Peggy turned
to her wordlessly.

"The telegram was phoned out shortly before you
came home. Your mother was resting, so I took the

message for her. I-I didn't give it to her until your aunt came home. Your uncle is making plane reservations for you to go home right now. I'm *so* sorry, Peggy." Then Aunt Emily hurried from the den and put her arms around Peggy.

"Don't bother packing any more than you need right now. We'll send the rest to you later. Your uncle has a plane reservation for you which will get you home by seven. He is going with you."

Peggy looked at her mother still standing rigidly in the hall and then back at her aunt uncertainly. "I don't think she'll want him to bother—"

"We won't ask her," Aunt Emily replied quietly. "He can see to things for you until your father gets home."

For the first time then the signature on the telegram registered on Peggy's consciousness and she looked at her aunt in sudden panic, whispering through lips that were stiff with fear, "The telegram was signed by Bob. He—he doesn't even mention Dad."

"That must mean he is all right. He probably asked Bob to send the telegram. Naturally the sender would automatically sign his own name." Then as Peggy continued to look at her pleadingly, Aunt Emily's lips trembled and she said, "Peggy, we *must* believe that until we hear differently." And Peggy knew her aunt was not really sure after all.

Jane tenderly put her arm around Peggy's shoulder. She prayed silently for God's grace for all, herself included.

Peggy looked down at the paper, and the words "Bill seriously injured—Bill seriously injured" were a broken record revolving endlessly in her mind. How seriously? Not daring to think what the words might mean, she buried her face in her hands to keep from seeing them. She couldn't break down, not if she were to be of any help to her mother.

"I know you think you can't eat anything," Peggy heard her aunt say. She sensed that she had turned to speak to Mrs. Andrews. Peggy raised her head and watched as her mother slowly turned from her frozen position and began to drag herself up the stairs, one step at a time, as though there were weights attached to her legs. Aunt Emily followed her progress with her eyes and said, "I'll send up a tray in a few minutes." Then she turned to Peggy. "You and Sally and Jane must come and eat something."

Peggy shuddered and could only shake her head, not daring to try to push words past her aching throat and trembling lips. But her aunt tightened her arms around her shoulders and said quietly, "Peggy, remember you have a guest here whom you invited for a special reason."

"But this—this changes everything!" Peggy gasped.

Aunt Emily spoke so that only Peggy could hear, and her voice was quiet and sure. "Do you think God didn't know Sally was to be here at the same time this other happened?"

At first Peggy's stunned mind and heart refused to take in the words. Then she lifted startled eyes to her aunt's face. This was in God's plan? Of course it was. And she knew Bill would be the first to say so. She didn't dare ask why about this; she had found so many times that God makes no mistakes. This was something she would have to hold onto when her mother's frozen

xterior began to crumble and she began to ask
uestions.

"Thank you, Aunt Emily," she whispered and turned
o Sally, who was still standing in the open doorway,
vatching and listening. Peggy glanced automatically
t her watch and couldn't believe it was only ten
ninutes after one. The last few minutes had seemed
ndless.

"I'm sorry," she began.

But Sally interrupted. "I'm the one who should be
orry for being in the way. Look, I don't have to stay
or dinner. Just let me use the phone and I'll call a
:ab—"

Aunt Emily interrupted firmly. "If you will all please
;o into the dining room and eat something, I'm sure
you'll be able to think more clearly. Sally, please stay.
You and Jane can help Peggy."

Sally turned to her, disbelief on her face. "Me?
How?"

"Just by being with her."

The rest of the hour passed in a blur. Peggy forced
food into her mouth and chewed and swallowed
mechanically, not tasting anything. She remembered
to call Ann and assured her Bob was all right and
promised to let her know any further details. She
made decisions about her clothes and her mother's
and worried about her mother who still sat motionless
in her room, staring straight ahead of her, seemingly
oblivious to what was going on. Peggy's concern looked
out of her eyes at her aunt though she didn't know
how to put her worry into words.

Aunt Emily shook her head in concern. Frowning,
she answered, "Perhaps she's better off like this. It

may be her way of taking the blow, and it will give her time to recover herself. Your uncle will help you with any problems so that your mother won't have to make any decisions until she is herself again."

"It's just—just that this is so unlike Mother. I've never known her to act like this."

"She's never had a shock like this before," her aunt replied. "Just be understanding, Peggy, if she finds it hard to accept—" She stopped and then finished soberly, "Whatever happens."

And Peggy nodded, sensing the thought her aunt did not want to put into words.

When it was almost time to leave for the airport, she took a last look around her room and then turned to Jane and Sally. "Thanks for helping."

She hugged Jane, who sobbed, "I wish I were going with you. The hardest part is waiting here and wondering what's happening."

Peggy was crying too as she answered, "I know. But then Aunt Emily would be all alone. We'll call the minute we know anything at all. Pray for Bill—and Dad—and especially Mother."

Peggy looked then at Sally, "I'm sorry. There are so many more things I wanted to talk to you about. And I want so much for you to know that I never intended to make you mad or drive you away from Christ."

Sally nodded back at Peggy's pleading look. "I'm not mad."

"I'm sure my aunt will have Roger take you back to your apartment when he comes back from the airport if you don't mind staying here until then."

"Don't worry about me, Peggy. You see, I'm going to—call my dad to get me and take me home."

"You mean really *home?*"

Sally nodded. "I had almost decided this a couple of days ago, especially after I found out that you and Jane had taken so much time to try to find me when I hadn't been very nice to you. But then, after you bawled me out, I was so mad that it made me too stubborn to do the thing that was for my own good. But today decided me for sure. This thing that's happened to you, I mean. I know how I would feel if one of the—the monsters got hurt and might not—" She looked at Peggy and Jane and then away without finishing the sentence.

"Anyway, this has made me realize how important a family is. And, Peggy, thanks. Lots of things you said years ago and just now outside make sense even though I don't understand them all yet—and some of them I'm not ready to accept either. But I want to."

She looked at Jane. "Maybe you can give me some help. And I know Mrs. Tremont will. And this time I'll make sure I know what I'm doing. I'll write you, Peggy. And I know I'll thank God many times for sending you here this month."

Peggy hugged Sally, crying again, and then hurried downstairs. Mrs. Andrews was already in the car, and Roger took Peggy's bag and put it in the trunk.

"Your uncle will be here in just a moment and you should have ample time to make the plane."

Peggy gave her aunt a last hug and whispered, "Thanks for everything. You've been wonderful. We'll call as soon as we can."

Her aunt hugged her back. "Remember, we are

praying together. This accident doesn't change our prayer for your mother at all."

She looked so confident that Peggy felt courage rising in her as it had never done before. Who was she to question God's working or His doing or His timing? The verse floated effortlessly to her mind, "How unsearchable are his judgments, and his ways past finding out!"

Peggy smiled back at her aunt through eyes that were wet with tears. It would be a sad journey and a hard time of waiting. But the end, whatever it was, would be glorious, because Bill's ways and her father's were committed to God. Her one responsibility was to help her mother see that no matter what the outcome was for Bill and Dad, she too must commit herself to God.